A Trademark Guide *for* Entrepreneurs

• *Kent Press* •

Stamford, Connecticut

A Trademark
Guide
for
Entrepreneurs

Robert E. Lee

Kent Communications, Ltd.
P.O. Box 1169
Stamford, Connecticut 06904-1169

Publisher's Cataloging in Publication
(Prepared by Quality Books Inc.)

Lee, Robert E., 1935-
A trademark guide for entrepreneurs / Robert E. Lee.
p. cm.
ISBN: 1-888206-05-5 (pbk.)
ISBN: 1-888206-04-7 (hc.)

1. Trademarks--United States--Law and legislation.   I. Title.
KF3180.L44 1996   346.7304'88
                                         QBI96-20395

To my sons,
Doug and Mike.

About the Author

Robert E. Lee has over thirty-five years of intellectual property law experience. During that time, he has negotiated more than 2,000 intellectual property agreements in over thirty-five countries. Mr. Lee's areas of expertise include copyrights, trademarks, patents, trade secrets, technology protection and licensing, copyright and trademark licensing, franchising, software agreements, research agreements, joint ventures and export control compliance and licensing.

Mr. Lee is registered to practice before the U.S. Patent and Trademark Office. He presently works for a major multi-national corporation where he has worldwide responsibility for trademarks and copyrights for the parent company and its subsidiaries and affiliates.

Mr. Lee has a J.D. Degree from Baylor University, an M.A. from Rice University and a B.S. from the University of Texas at Austin. He is a member of the State Bar of Texas, where he scored the highest grade on the bar examination. He is a trustee of the Citizens' Scholarship Foundation of America, Inc. and is a trademark and copyright advisor to the Community Redevelopment Agency of the City of Los Angeles. Mr. Lee is a long-time member of the Licensing Executives Society (LES) and the International Trademark Association (INTA). Mr. Lee resides in Plano, Texas.

Table of Contents

Preface

Every business has at least one thing in common, a trade name or business name. A business has to have a name to operate under, to put on stationery, and to list in the phone book. Most businesses also have trademarks and service marks, although the proprietors might not know it. Some businesses have entire portfolios of valuable trademarks (their proverbial "family jewels").

Despite the importance of trademarks and trade names, few managers, owners or entrepreneurs understand how to use or protect them. Substantive courses on the practical use of trademarks and trade names aren't taught in business or graduate school. And even if they were, trademark law has changed dramatically since 1989, and the business community needs to be updated on the new rights and opportunities that are available.

Trademarks have become an offensive force, and should be used aggressively, rather than merely as a defensive shield. "Intent to use" trademark applications provide a means to acquire rights to marks and names *before* they are used or disclosed. This is worth repeating: *rights can be acquired before use or public disclosure.*

Unregistered trademarks, designs, and trade dress are protected under federal unfair competition law, and the basis for false advertising actions has been broadened. And a federal trademark dilution statute has been passed.

Corporate officers, directors, and managers; sole proprietors; partners; joint venturers; directors of organizations; individuals forming businesses; attorneys, accountants, marketing and name consultants; and advertising executives, to name a few, will find ample topics of interest. And for the entrepreneur, there are many intriguing avenues to explore.

The entrepreneur and trademarks were made for each other. With trademarks you can get into business literally on a shoestring without having any assets other than a priority right to a name or mark. What this allows you to do is create a product or service which is identified with the name or mark. Can a trademark carry a business with it? You bet. Come up with the right trademark, and you can create a business around it.

One

Overview of Trademark Law

This chapter reviews the fundamental concepts of trademarks and discusses rules for using and registering them. Trademarks, service marks and trade names surround us. Any entrepreneur who starts a business, sells a product or provides a service has rights to the names or marks that are used. Federal and state trademark and service mark registrations can be obtained. "Intent to use" federal trademark and service mark applications can be filed to reserve marks *before* use or marketing. Trade dress, trade names and unregistered trademarks are protected, and a federal cause of action exists for false advertising. Famous marks are federally protected from dilution.

COMMON LAW DERIVATION

As with many of our laws, trademarks and trade names rights derive from common law.[1] Early-on, it was established that a name or symbol used by a person to designate and operate his business, or to mark or distinguish his products, should be protected. The owner developed rights to trade names and trademark rights which could exclude use by others.

> **TERMS AND REFERENCES**
>
> The term "trademarks" often refers to both trademarks and service marks. The author has followed this practice, except where the context clearly indicates otherwise. "Marks" mean trademarks and service marks. "Names" mean trade names. The same word can be both a mark and a name. Unless otherwise indicated, all section references are to the Lanham Act. "Rule" refers to the Trademark Rules of Practice.

---

[1] In civil law countries, there are no common law rights since all rights are statutory.

Eventually, it was recognized that trade names and trademarks represented property rights which could be sold or inherited when the goodwill of the business was transferred with them. Transferring both the mark and the goodwill associated with the mark provided the assurance that the public would receive the same quality of goods or products after the transfer occurred.

Goodwill and consistent quality came to be associated with trademarks and trade names, and these concepts have become the keystones of modern trademarks. How often have you heard that a trademark cannot be assigned without goodwill, or that a trademark owner must exercise quality control? These statements are more than lip service, and the trademark rights may be lost if these rules are ignored

STATUS OF MARKS AND NAMES TODAY

Common law trademarks and trade names are still around, since common law rights are not pre-empted by state and federal trademark statutes. If a seller sells a product under a selected brand name, or operates a business under a trade name, that seller has common law rights. These rights exist independently of any registrations or name recordals.[2]

Common law trademarks (or, for that matter, any rights acquired through registration) are *usage based*. If the seller stops using the trade name or selling products under the trademarks for an extended period with no intention of resuming, his or her trademark rights will be abandoned. Trademarks depend on public recognition and perception and have a short "half-life" when left on the shelf.[3]

Protection for trademarks under common law has limitations. Common law trademarks and trade names are territori-

---

[2] In fact, the registrations are a redundancy, since you would still have common law rights — assuming your use had been continuous — if the federal or state registrations lapse.

[3] What if you cease using a mark, but still have a registration? The registration is a piece of paper, that's all. You might as well make a paper airplane with it and sail it across the room. If you start use of the mark again, your priority rights start anew and you can not tack on the first date of use claimed in the registration.

ally restricted. If a seller operates statewide, then he or she has statewide common law rights. If the seller markets in a single city, and does not advertise over a wider area, then rights will likely be limited to that city. Common law trademarks protect the seller, but only for the territory of use and for the same or similar goods or services. Also, common law rights relate only to the seller's *particular* products or business activity. For example, if a seller uses "ACE" as a mark for computers, that seller cannot expect to block a subsequent vendor who is selling "ACE" transmissions.

Sellers cannot expect much protection if they are using names or marks which are descriptive of their goods and services. For example, if "Speedy's Bikes" is used as the name of a bicycle shop, the shop owner cannot expect to prevent "SPEEDY" from being used by a manufacturer as a trademark for bicycles. The name is too descriptive.

There are disadvantages to relying on common law rights for trademark protection. While common law rights are automatic, their scope of protection is limited, they are difficult to enforce and distinctiveness (secondary meaning) must be shown. Nevertheless, the rights are free and should not be overlooked.

THE CONSTITUTION AND USE IN COMMERCE

Under the Constitution, Congress has the power to regulate commerce with foreign nations, among the states, and with Indian tribes.[4] It is the right to control commerce that gives Congress the power to pass trademark legislation.[5]

"Commerce" is defined as follows: ". . . all commerce which may lawfully be regulated by Congress."[6] In the case of trademarks, this isn't much of a stretch, since trademarks and the flow of goods in commerce go hand in hand. And the courts seem willing to find commerce in almost every situation.[7]

---

[4] Article I, Section 8, Clause 3.
[5] Patents and copyrights have a directly supporting section in the Constitution so that a commerce connection is not required.
[6] §45 of the Lanham Act.
[7] Purely intrastate commerce which affects other controlled commerce is sufficient for jurisdictional basis. *Larry Harmon Pictures Corp. v. Williams Restaurant Corp.*, 929 F.2d 662 (Fed, Cir. 1991)

Historically, in order to file an application for a trademark, the mark had to be used on products or goods being sold or transported, or in connection with the services being provided, in *interstate* or *foreign* commerce. If there was no use, or if use was purely intrastate, the underlying statutory requirement was not met and an application could not be filed.

TOKEN USE IS PASSÉ

Prior to the 1988 Amendment to the Lanham Act, token use was accepted as use in commerce for filing purposes, provided the applicant followed through in a reasonable time with actual commercial use. Before filing the application, the seller would have to make a couple of sales in interstate commerce. However, with the adoption of intent to use filings in 1988, actual use is no longer necessary to file, and token use was discarded. When proof of use is provided, it has to be legitimate bona fide use. "Use in commerce" must be made in ordinary trade and not merely to reserve a mark.

With the advent of "intent to use" (ITU) trademark applications, the concept of use has been significantly expanded. A legal presumption is made that there is *constructive* use of the mark for the claimed goods or services when an applicant files on an intent to use basis on the Principal Register. Use in commerce is still required before a registration can issue, except that now, use can be delayed until *after* the trademark has been examined and published.

With intent to use applications, the applicant gets territorial preemption as of the *date of filing* for the goods and services covered by the registration for the entire United States. This means an applicant can, without having actual use, file for whatever goods or services he or she wants to cover (has intent to use) and obtain priority over subsequent actual users.[8]

---

[8] Under pre-1988 law, an applicant had to use the mark in commerce and then file an application. The filing date had little significance since it was the first use date and the registration date which were important.

EVOLUTION OF TRADEMARKS

Trademarks and service marks were defined in 1946 as follows. A "trademark" was: "... any word, name, symbol, or device or any combination thereof, adopted and used by a manufacturer or merchant to identify his goods and distinguish them from those manufactured or sold by others." And a "service mark" was: ". . . a mark used in the sale or advertising of services to identify the services of one person and distinguish them from the services of others." [9]

These are familiar standard definitions. The new definitions, which include additions to account for intent to use, are found in Chapter Three. However, the above definitions are the easiest to study.

FEDERAL AND STATE TRADEMARKS

State and federal trademark registrations are obtained by filing applications with the U.S. Patent and Trademark Office and the respective secretaries of state. Both state and federal grants of trademark rights are represented by registration certificates.[10] Each registered trademark has to be prepared, filed and prosecuted individually.[11]

This, however, is where the similarities between federal and state grants end. The rights granted to an owner with state registrations are insignificant compared to the rights of a federal registration. State grants usually are no better than a party's common law trademark rights. The federal grants are substantial and go well beyond anything at common law.

Typically, a trademark owner will possess a combination of common law, state and federal rights, which can be collectively

---

[9] For the first time in American law, the 1946 Lanham Act provided for the registration of service marks.

[10] Common law rights have to be proven by introducing evidence in court of use. State and federal trademarks are evidenced by certificates of registration.

[11] It would be great if a company could file a single application for all its trademarks. This would save the Patent and Trademark Office the expense of making individual examinations. To keep the applicant from overreaching, an annual maintenance fee could be required.

or selectively enforced. This allows the trademark owner to pick and choose when bringing legal action.[12]

ADVANTAGES OF FEDERAL TRADEMARKS

The following is a partial listing of advantages for federal trademark registration holders:
(1) Federal registrations cover all of the U.S. and its possessions.
(2) Priority rights relate to the date of filing.
(3) Federal registrations on the Principal Register can become incontestable after time.
(4) Significant penalties are provided against infringers.
(5) Statutory notice is given of registrations.
(6) "Intent to use" filings are permitted.
(7) Federal registrations are presumed to be valid.
(8) Federal registrations can be the basis of foreign applications.
(9) States are precluded from modifying registered marks.
(10) Federal registrations can be recorded with Customs to prevent imports.
(11) An official register is kept of title (assignments).
(12) Supplemental registrations are available.

The Lanham Act, which became effective July 5, 1947, defines federal trademark law. While there have been numerous amendments to the Lanham Act, the 1988 Amendment, which became effective November 16, 1989, is the most significant. In the 1988 Act, filing on the Principal Register on an "intent to use" basis was legally equated with actual use. Therefore, priority rights to a trademark can be established by filing an intent to use application on the Principal Register, subject to subsequent use in commerce.[13]

---

[12] State and common law claims can be combined with a federal cause of action.

[13] There are time limits, and if the applicant does not use the mark in commerce within the permitted time, the application will lapse and the applicant will lose the priority date. The applicant can file again and start over with a new date, if nobody has intervened.

43(a) — A SECTION TO REMEMBER

In addition to providing for intent to use applications, a second major change made by the 1988 Act was to expand Section 43(a). This has become a general federal law of unfair competition. Under Section 43(a), a trademark owner can sue in federal court for trade dress infringement, or for infringement of unregistered trademarks, service marks or commercial activities. Also, new claims can be made for false advertising under this provision. The 1988 Act clarified that damages for Section 43(a) actions are those damages normally available for trademark infringement.

TRADE NAMES

Trade or business names can take many forms. They can be corporate names, partnership names, joint venture names, organizational names, dba's for individuals or divisional or unit names, etc. Almost any name that is tagged on a business, including acronyms and truncated versions of official names, is a trade name. Trade names are associated with the business as a whole, rather than relating to a particular product or service.

For example, assume that "Planet Gasoline Company," a.k.a. "Big Sky," sells "BLAST-OFF" brand gasoline and uses "BLAST-OFF" with the design of a rocket on its sign and in advertising. "Planet Gasoline Company" is the corporate name. "Planet Gasoline" and "Big Sky" are trade names. "BLAST-OFF" is a trademark and service mark. "The Rocket design" is a service mark.

Corporations, or other formal forms of business organizations, such as partnerships, have a home state where they are incorporated or organized. The states approve and register the official business names of the legal entities organized within the states and foreign entities that want to qualify to do business.

These recordal statutes were designed to keep other parties from adopting and recording similar names and to provide minimal defensive name protection.[14] Many states have fictitious, or

---

[14] It usually is not a factor that the respective businesses are similar or dissimilar.

assumed name statutes, whose purpose is to identify the party behind a name. These generally do not protect the names from use by others.

How then, are trade names protected? I wish I could say you could federally register them, but the Lanham Act does not provide a mechanism for registering trade names, even though they are protected under Section 43(a).

End of story? No, it is just the beginning. Wherever there are rules, there are exceptions. While a trade name cannot be registered *per se* under the Lanham Act, the principal word or words in a trade name can be registered as trademarks or service marks if that is how they are used. In the example given above, if "PLANET" or "BIG SKY" is used on the pump dispensers, this is trademark use and the mark would be registrable.

QUALITY CONTROL AND CONSISTENCY

Quality control and consistency of products and services are hallmarks of trademark protection. A purchaser should be able to go into any store and acquire a brand named product with the assurance that the quality of the product will be consistent regardless of the place of purchase. If consumers go to "Outrageous Burger Drive-ins" in Dallas, they would expect to be offered the same choice of food items and receive the same level of service that they would in restaurants in Los Angeles. Similarly, consumers can shop for the best price on a "ROLEX" watch at various locations worldwide with the assurance that any watch they purchase will have the same fine quality and level of performance. Even if the consumer does not know what company produces "ROLEX" watches, it is assumed that a unitary source exists which oversees the quality.

Where the trademark owner is manufacturing and selling the trademarked products, quality control is immediate and direct, and the owner is responsible for the resulting goodwill or lack thereof. The same situation applies to wholly-owned subsidiaries; under the Lanham Act, they are statutorily considered to be "related companies." However, affiliates which are less than 100 percent-owned fall under a different rule. In this case, direct quality control is required by the parent company. Therefore, the parent company should issue a written license to the affiliate, which includes quality control provisions, as well as provisions for actual on-site control or monitoring.

Another area where quality control is required is licensing unrelated third parties. Unless the licensor sets standards for the trademark-bearing goods and services manufactured by the licensee and ensures that certain standards are followed, the goodwill associated with the trademark may be affected. Failure by a trademark owner to exercise quality control over its own goods and services can result in abandonment of the trademark. Similarly, if the trademark owner fails to control the quality of goods or services of subsidiaries, affiliates, licensees or franchisees, the trademark may be found to have been abandoned.

GOODWILL

Under U.S. law, goodwill and trademarks are irrevocably married to each other. Divorce or annulment is not possible. Trademarks and service marks are encased in an invisible envelope of goodwill and cannot be assigned independently.[15] The value of the goodwill usually increases with use, advertising, sales, consumer acceptance and quality of products or services. However, goodwill is fragile, since any negative association with the source of the goods or services can destroy or severely damage the goodwill.

The trademark owner must be diligent in protecting the goodwill associated with a mark from infringement or encroachment by others. If the trademark owner allows third parties to use a mark to produce inferior products, or provide inferior services, the mark may be found to be abandoned.

Likewise, the sale of a trade name with an ongoing business requires a transfer of goodwill. With a stock sale, this is easy, since when stock is being transferred, all other rights go with it. With an asset sale, the goodwill applicable to the business being sold, e.g., equipment, supplies, etc., should be transferred, if possible. If the business is goes bankrupt and is being liquidated,

---

[15] §10 requires that "part of the goodwill of the business connected with the use of and symbolized by the mark" be transferred.

whether the rights to a name or mark can be assigned is problematic.

RULES OF USAGE

Trademarks have basic rules of usage that should always be followed. Any written correspondence or advertising copy concerning the trademark should be devised carefully, keeping in mind these rules of usage. Trademarks are proper adjectives, meaning that the initial letter of each word should be capitalized. Alternatively, all letters of a mark can be capitalized, or the trademark used in a special form. Being a proper adjective, the trademark should modify a noun when used in a sentence, which is generic or descriptive of the product or service.[16] If the mark is frequently used as a noun and not an adjective, it may become generic and be dedicated to the public.[17]

Just as consistency of products and services is required, there should also be consistency of *the form* (appearance) of the trademark. Trademarks must comply with design standards and should not be varied and used in different ways. If a trademark is used inconsistently, or improperly, the public will become confused as to its source of origin, and the trademark may be jeopardized.

NOTICE OF REGISTRATION

The traditional form of trademark notice is the ® or "Circle R" symbol. Alternative notice forms are: "Registered in U.S. Patent and Trademark Office," or "Reg. U.S., Pat. & Tm. Off." These notices should only be used for federal registrations on

---

[16] The reference noun can be varied so long as it fits the product or service. For example, a particular organic chemical reactant could be referred to by its official chemical name, or by various generic names, e.g., polyol, reactant, material, compound, etc.

[17] For most trademark owners, this is not going to be a viable danger. However, even if the mark is not at risk, the trademark owner's lack of proper policing is likely to show up during discovery during enforcement proceedings. If a trademark is on a product or container, it is usually considered that the product represents the generic name and an additional written name is unnecessary.

the Supplemental and Principal Registers of the U.S. Patent and Trademark Office.

There is no requirement that a trademark notice be used, and there are no penalties for its non-use. However, *no recovery can be made for profits and damages* if there is no trademark notice. The logic is that if there is no notice, the defendant has no knowledge of infringement. But, don't jump the gun and use a notice too soon! If a trademark owner uses the "Circle R" notice before the actual registration date, the registration could be held unenforceable because of misuse.

TERM OF TRADEMARKS

How long do trademarks last? Federal registrations have ten-year renewable terms, as do most state and foreign marks.[18] As a result, trademarks can go on forever, assuming that use of the mark continues, and timely renewals are made.[19]

STATE TRADEMARKS

All states have trademark laws, and most follow the Model Act. State trademarks do not cost much nor do they offer much in the way of rights. Why obtain them? One reason would be if the seller is not engaged in Interstate Commerce. Another reason is to be able to list a registration in the franchise offering circular. It is often the case that the people who file for state registrations do not know how to obtain federal rights.

FEDERAL UNFAIR COMPETITION

In 1988, Section 43(a) of the Lanham Act was amended to cover (1) claims for false designations of origin and (2) false advertising. The false designation of origin claims can be used to bring actions for infringement of unregistered trademarks, trade names and trade dress. The false advertising causes of action are available to those who can show they were directly harmed, and include false claims by the advertiser, both about his or her

---

[18] Proof of use is required to renew federal registrations.

[19] For example, the "DU PONT" name and mark has continued generation after generation since the 18th Century.

product, service or commercial activities, *or false claims about the plaintiff's.*

TRADEMARK ANTI-DILUTION

On January, 16, 1996, President Clinton signed legislation creating an anti-dilution trademark statute. This protects against the collateral use of "famous" trademarks under circumstances where there is no competition between the parties. Therefore, federal protection now exists for a mark outside its primary field of use.

For instance, the famous mark "MERCEDES" would be protected against use on products unrelated to automobiles, such as pianos or guitars. This expansion of trademark rights is a boon to the trademark owner, since licensing possibilities will increase. The kicker is that most entrepreneurs are not going to be starting with famous marks.

TYPICAL TRADEMARK SCENARIOS

1. Red sells "ACE" gadgets in Dallas. Red will have common law rights to "ACE" as a trademark for gadgets, and will be able to prevent others from marketing "ACE" gadgets in Dallas or its vicinity. However, unless Red is selling gadgets nationwide, there will be geographic gaps in his rights. Thus, Red will be unable to stop a party, who had no notice of Red's prior operations, from selling "ACE" gadgets in other market territories.

2. Mary Jane, who is in the mail order business, wants to offer a new line of designer watches. She comes up with the trademark "NIFTY," and files an intent to use federal application on "NIFTY" on the Principal Register for watches in Int. Class 14 (the class for jewelry and watches.) A competitor learns of Mary Jane's plans and begins marketing watches under the mark first. Who has priority? Mary Jane will, once her application issues, since filing on an ITU basis on the Principal Register is constructive use.

3. Joe, who is in the canoe and raft rental business, incorpo-

rates under the name "Boat'n Float, Inc. Joe starts business and two years pass. He receives notification from Lost Land Ventures (LLV), which conducts river rafting trips, that he is infringing their federal trademark registration for BOAT AND FLOAT for transportation and entertainment services in the nature of guided canoe trips. LLV's trademark application was filed on the Principal Register before Joe started business. Joe explains that he was granted rights to the corporate name. However, federal rights are overriding, and if LLV performs services under its mark in the same market territory as Joe, Joe will have to cease business or change names.

CROSS REFERENCES

Chapter Two lists names that cannot be trademarks. Chapter Three discusses the types of trademarks and shows how they are characterized and grouped.

Two

Exclusions from Registration

A trademark or service mark is "a word, name, symbol or device, or any combination thereof by which the goods or services of the applicant may be distinguished from the goods or services of others."[1] It is fundamental, therefore, that trademarks relate to particular goods or services, since otherwise, there is nothing to identify and distinguish. An owner who is looking to choose a trademark or business name cannot conduct a meaningful search, thereby eliminating unregistrable names, until the owner knows what the products or services will be.

Advertisers love descriptive trademarks because they get the advertising campaign off to a fast start, since purchasers understand them. If the promotion has little long-term potential, this is fine. However, when the product or service is envisioned to have staying power, the owner will want a mark that people will not tire of and one that is arbitrary so that it can be registered on the Principal Register in the U.S. Patent and Trademark Office.

Since there is no pre-approved list of names to choose trademarks from, the owner has to work in reverse and determine what names *cannot* be trademarked. Then, every other name, device or symbol which qualifies as a trademark, including invented or coined names, is up for grabs.

There are two federal registers for filing trademark applications — the Principal Register and the Supplemental Register. The Principal Register is where applicants want to be; the Supplemental Register is where they end up by default when their marks are descriptive. The Principal Register gives the applicant a number of advantages over common law trademarks, including statutory notice, territorial pre-emption, a presumption

[1] §2

15

of validity and the possibility of the registration becoming incontestable after five years of continuous use. The Supplemental Register is for marks which are *capable* of distinguishing the applicant's goods or services, but which currently fail the test. Marks on the Supplemental Register receive registration numbers, can be used by examiners as references and even get to sport the "Circle R."[2]

The Lanham Act and other federal statutes exclude certain names from being trademarks. The first part of this chapter lists the types of marks which are excluded from registration on the Principal and Supplemental Registers. The second part lists the types of names which are precluded from the Principal Register, but which are registrable on the Supplemental Register. The third part of this chapter is a common sense list of names and devices which cannot be trademarks. Take away these exceptions, and all other names are potentially available.

MARKS EXCLUDED FROM THE PRINCIPAL AND SUPPLEMENTAL REGISTERS

Immoral, Deceptive or Scandalous Marks

Registration is precluded for a trademark which:

Consists of or comprises immoral, deceptive, or scandalous matter; or matter which may disparage or falsely suggest a connection with persons, living or dead, institutions, beliefs, or national symbols, or bring them into contempt, or disrepute. [3]

Examples of marks refused registration hereunder include: BULLSHIT for T-shirts (held profane) and a graphic of a dog defecating for T-shirts (held scandalous). In contrast, a condom

---

[2] Supplemental registrations look like the real thing, however, their rights are restricted. They have no notice or pre-emptive effect and are not presumed to be valid. Intent to use procedures cannot be used with them and they cannot become incontestable.

[3] §2(a) of the Lanham Act.

decorated with stars and strips so as to suggest the American flag was not considered scandalous.[4]

Flags, Coats of Arms and Insignias

Registration is precluded for a trademark which: "Consists of or comprises the flag or coat of arms or other insignia of the United States, or any state or municipality, or of any foreign nation, or simulation thereof."[5] Condoms with the British flag, or the Rising Sun, probably would be excluded under this provision. Therefore, it may be best to forget any marketing scheme that includes flags of the countries, since it would not be protectable.

Names, Portraits or Signatures of Living Individuals

Registration is precluded for a trademark which:

Consists of or comprises a name, portrait, or signature, identifying a particular living individual except by his written consent, or the name, signature, or portrait of a deceased President of the United States during the life of his widow, if any, except by written consent of the widow.[6]

Since most names could be the name of someone, does this mean that the applicant must run around the country getting consents? If the applicant represents that the name is fictitious, it can be used, irrespective of whether it is someone's name.[7]

Confusingly Similar Marks or Names

Registration is denied where a trademark:

---

[4] As the cases indicate, whether a mark will be registered is unpredictable. It will depend on the product, the examiner and public acceptance of the product.

[5] §2(b)

[6] §2(c)

[7] However, the applicant will not be allowed to purposely play on someone's name.

Consists of or comprises a mark which so resembles a mark previously registered in the Patent and Trademark Office, or a mark or trade name previously used in the United States by another and not abandoned, as to be likely, when used on or in connection with the goods of the applicant, to cause confusion, or to cause mistake, or to deceive. [8]

Note that this definition includes trade names and trademarks in the U.S., as well as federally registered marks. However, the examiner only searches for confusingly similar *federally registered* marks. This does not mean that state trademarks and trade names are not pertinent, since they are legitimate references and often come into play in oppositions, cancellations and in determining the validity of the trademark.

Registration depends on the *likelihood of confusion* as to the *source* or *origin* of goods. Each case must be decided on its own facts. When there is doubt, the decision is against the newcomer. Third party registrations can be used to show that a reference only has a narrow field. Where two or more pending applications appear to conflict, the earlier case is published so the other parties can oppose.[9]

Geographically Deceptively Misdescriptive Marks

Registration is refused where the mark is primarily "geographically deceptively misdescriptive" of applicant's goods.[10] Names which are geographically deceptively misdescriptive are disqualified from either register. NAFTA reinforced this requirement. However, the exclusion does not apply to marks which became distinctive before the date of enactment of NAFTA. (In a related matter, GATT required the U.S. to amend Section 2 to preclude registration of geographic indications of wine and spirits.)

---

[8] §2(d)

[9] Where two applications have the same filing date, the one with the lower serial number will control.

[10] §2(e)(3)

CONFUSINGLY SIMILAR

If two marks are similar in appearance, sound or meaning, they are confusingly similar. In applying the above tests, all one has to prove is a *likelihood* of confusion. Side by side comparisons are not allowed, and purchasers are not required to have perfect recall.

Of course, close relation of the products or services is required, since even for identical marks there would be no confusion for totally dissimilar products. Thus, there would not likely be any confusion between "JUMP START" as a mark for handguns and for bar glasses. However, items which fall under the same generic heading will be considered to be related. Hence, "THE EDGE" as a mark for caps and for T-shirts would be confusingly similar since they are both clothing items.

Statutorily Protected Names

Apart from the Lanham Act, numerous federal statutes have been passed to prohibit or restrict the use of certain words, names and symbols used by agencies of the U.S. Government, by veteran and youth organizations, by international organizations and for the humanities, health, education and welfare, etc.

The Paris Convention Restrictions

The U.S. is a member of the Paris Convention, which makes the Paris Convention part of the U.S. law. Under Article 6*ter* of the Paris Convention treaty, contracting countries have agreed to refuse to register as trademarks armorial bearings, flags, emblems, etc., of the member countries.

Varietal and Cultivar Names

The generic names of plants and seeds by which the varieties are known to the public can not be trademarked.[11] An example is Acer sacccharum for red maple.

---

[11] Manual of Trademark Examining Procedure, 1202.05

STATUTORY EXCLUSIONS

All statutory restrictions of names that can not be trademarked are not in the Lanham Act. The following is a sample listing of names which are precluded by specific act of Congress:
• Designations associated with the Olympics, e.g., "Olympic," "Olympiad," and "Citrus Altius Fortius";
• the Greek Red Cross other than by the American National Red Cross;
• "Copyright," "Copr.," the letter "C" in a circle, the letter "P" in a circle, the symbol "*M*," or letter "M" in a circle;
• the Civil Air Patrol;
• the American Legion;
• the Blinded Veterans Association;
• Future Farmers of America and "FFA";
• Girl Scouts of America;
• Little League Baseball;
• Smoky Bear;
• Woodsy Owl;
• USO;
• 4-H Club;
• National Safety Council.

MARKS EXCLUDED FROM THE PRINCIPAL REGISTER

The following types of marks are excluded from the Principal Register, without a showing of secondary meaning, but qualify for the Supplemental Register, if they are capable of distinguishing the applicant's goods or services.

The Lanham Act carves out a wide territory for obtaining registrations on the Supplemental Register:[12] "any trademark, symbol, label, package, configuration, of goods, name, word, slogan, phrase, surname, geographic name, numeral, or device or any combination of the foregoing." This list not only includes items which would pose problems on the Principal Register with-

---

[12] §23(c)

out a showing of secondary meaning, e.g., surnames, geographic names, etc., but also includes leading edge stuff, like "configuration of goods."

WARNING: The Supplemental Register cannot be used for intent to use applications. If you file an intent to use based application on the Supplemental Register, it will be returned.[13]

Descriptive or Deceptively Misdescriptive Marks

The Lanham Act precludes registration on the Principal Register of: "marks which are 'merely descriptive of' or 'deceptively misdescriptive of' the goods of the applicant."[14] Trademarks which describe some characteristic of the goods are descriptive. However, deceptively misdescriptive goes a step further. Inferring a characteristic to the goods which they do not have, for a deceptive purpose, is using deceptive intent. For example, "CLEAN AIR" for cigarettes would likely be deceptively misdescriptive.

Geographically Descriptive Marks

Terms which are descriptive of a geographic location, or origin of goods and services, are not considered inherently distinctive.[15] Therefore, secondary meaning is required for the Principal Register. Registration is permitted on the Supplemental Register. For example, while an applicant may be unable to register "TEXAS" for chili, he or she could probably register it on the Supplemental Register.

Marks Which are Primarily Surnames

The Lanham act precludes the registration of marks which are primarily surnames on the Principal Register without proof of secondary meaning.[16]

---

[13] At one time a mark had to be used for a year before it could be put on the Supplemental Register, but this restriction was lifted and application can be made anytime there has been use.

[14] Section 2(e)(1)

[15] ibid.

[16] ibid.

MISCELLANEOUS EXCLUSIONS

The following is a non-statutory listing of names and things that logically cannot be trademarks.

Generic Names

Generic names for the concerned goods and services cannot be trademarked on either register. They are in the public domain and available for use by anyone. It makes no difference that alternative generic names are available. A door is a door and cannot be a trademark for a portal. "Spectacles" cannot be a trademark for eye glasses. "Cutting Tool" cannot be a trademark for knives.[17]

Ornamental Designs

If a design is *solely* ornamental and decorative, it is not separately registrable on either register. An example would be wallpaper in a restaurant. It used to be that designs on T-shirts were routinely rejected on this basis. But now it is accepted that a mark does not have to indicate the manufacturer, and items of clothing sporting various logos have become the most important product merchandising licensing class.

Functionality Exclusions

The biggest problem associated with trademarking product containers is functionality.[18] If a feature is functional, it cannot be trademarked. If a design is non-functional or *de facto* functional, it may be registrable. *De facto* functional designs require proof of secondary meaning and may be placed on the Supplemental Register. *De jure* functional means that a configuration is

---

[17] However, "Cutting Tool" could be used as a mark for other products where it is arbitrary, e.g., "Cutting Tool" rubber water hose or "Cutting Tool" computer chips.

[18] A functional feature has been defined as one which is essential to the use or purpose of the article or affects its cost or quality. *Inwood Laboratories, Inc. v. Ives Laboratories , Inc.*, 486 U.S. 844, n.10, 214 USPQ 1 (1982).

deemed by law to be functional and cannot be registered on either register.[19]

Product designs which have been registered include: the round thermostat cover used by Honeywell and a kettle and legs arrangement for a barbecue grill. The Haig pinched decanter is a classic example of a design which is trademarked.[20]

Trade Names

The Lanham Act defines trade names and trademarks, and yet trade names are not registrable, since no provision says that they are. Therefore, names which are *merely* trade names are refused registration. However, if a trade name functions as a trademark or service mark, it may be registrable. Since the same word or words can be a trade name, a trademark and a service mark depending on how they are used, a case by case determination is necessary.[21]

Style and Grade Designations

Words, numbers and symbols which do not identify and distinguish the goods but only designate grade, style or quality are not trademarks. These kind of designations are considered descriptive. An example of a grade designation is "10W-30 for motor oil."

Contests and Promotional Services

Using a contest to promote the sale of one's own goods is not considered to be a service, and the name of the contest would not be registrable. If the name is used to promote the sale of goods or services of others, then the contest name would be registrable as advertising.

---

[19] At one time there were cases that used the term "aesthetic functionality." This concept of ornamentation functionality has been rejected by the courts.

[20] *Ex parte Haig & Haig Ltd.*, 118 USPQ 229,230, (Comm'r. Pats. 1958)

[21] If a name is used with an address, it will normally be considered as a trade name.

Processes, Systems or Methods

A process is not considered a service because it is a way of doing something. Therefore, the name of a process is not a service mark. However, the name of a petrochemical process is registrable as a service mark, if service mark usage can be shown.[22]

Geographic Indication of Wines and Spirits

A geographic indication which, when used on or in connection with wines or spirits, identifies a place other than the origin of the goods and is first used on or in connection with wines or spirits by the applicant on or after one year after the date on which the WPO agreement enters force in the U.S. cannot be registered as a mark. Section 2 (a) of the Lanham Act. This provision became effective January 1, 1996 and precludes registration on either the Principal or Supplemental Registers of qualifying geographic indications.

CROSS REFERENCES

Chapters Three and Four provide information on how to search and select trade names and trademarks. Chapters Five, Six and Seven cover filing and prosecuting federal trademark applications.

---

[22] The trick is to identify the process name with a particular service. For example, consulting or technical assistance could be provided under the name.

Three

Types and Styles of Marks

As mandated by the Lanham Act, there are four general types of statutory marks — trademarks, service marks, certification marks and collective marks. Many other forms and types of marks could have been characterized in the Lanham Act but were not.[1] The statutory definitions of "trademark," "service mark" and "certification mark" state that they can be any word, name, symbol, or device or any combination thereof.[2]

At one time a product was limited to a single trademark, since there was a single manufacturer producing it, but this restriction is gone. Under a "source of origin" concept, which now prevails, it is generally accepted that with quality control, there can be multiple manufacturers or providers of goods or services. In addition, a manufacturer can use primary and secondary marks, "house marks" and third party "endorsement" marks. Trademarks can also be used in combination with one another or with non-trademark components.

You can register trademarks in block letters and in stylized or logo form. You can register the same form of mark for different goods and services. You can register marks in color (as lined drawings) and black and white. You can register a composite form of the mark and then separately register any individual elements which make a separate visual impression.

---

[1] If the Trademark Act had been written in a comprehensive form like the Copyright Act, a dozen or more types of marks could easily have been defined.

[2] A collective mark was not included, since it is defined as a trademark, service mark or certification mark.

STATUTORILY RECOGNIZED TYPES OF MARKS

Certification Marks

Certification marks are marks used by someone *other than the owner* to certify regional or other origin, material, mode of manufacture, union labor, etc. The owner of the mark must not produce the goods or perform the services. An example of a certification mark is the UL standard of quality for Underwriters Laboratories.[3] Another well-known example is the Good House Keeping Seal of Approval. Certification marks can be applied for based on intent to use the mark.

Collective Marks

Collective marks cover members of organizations, cooperatives, etc. Because they have little application to this book, they are not discussed further. Intent to use filings are available for these types of marks.

Trademarks

A "trademark" is defined in the 1988 Amendment to the Lanham Act as:

> . . . any word, name, symbol, or device, or any combination thereof —
> (1) used by a person, or
> (2) which a person has a bona fide intention to use in commerce and applies to register on the principal register established by this Act,
> to identify and distinguish his or her goods, including a unique product, from those manufactured or sold by others and to indicate the source of goods, even if that source is unknown.[4]

---

[3] Roofing material, for example, is UL certified for degree of resistance to external fire and flammability limits and degree of wind resistance.

[4] §45 of the Lanham Act

As is obvious from the definition, "intent to use" is a significant aspect of the law. Intent to use has been equated with actual use so far as establishing a priority date goes. A trademark is a mark which is either in use, or which a person has a bona fide *intention to use* in commerce.

While this seemingly runs contrary to the use in commerce requirement, the Lanham Act couples the intent to use requirement with the tangible act of applying to register a trademark on the Principal Register. Then, trademark registration is not granted until the applicant actually submits proof of use in commerce. Use in commerce is still required, only now it has been deferred.

Service Marks

A "service mark" is defined as:

... any word, name, symbol, or device, or any combination thereof —
(1) used by a person, or
(2) which a person has a bona fide intention to use in commerce and applies to register on the principal register established by this Act,
to identify and distinguish the services of one person, including a unique service, from the services of others and to indicate the source of the services, even if that source is unknown.[5]

Titles, character names, and other distinctive features of radio or television programs may be registered as service marks notwithstanding that they, or the programs, may advertise goods of a sponsor.

Service marks did not exist at common law and were included in the Lanham Act as an afterthought. "Service," like "fair use" under the copyright laws, was never clearly defined and has created a veil of uncertainty.

---

[5] ibid.

RETAIL SALES

Retail sales qualify as services and are registrable with the U.S. Patent and Trademark Office, which is contrary to the position in most other countries. The U.S. seems to be on its own in this regard. Other countries limit services to where actual personal services are performed for the customer e.g., restaurant services, hotel services, photography services, auto repair services, barber and beauty shop services, etc.

The Patent and Trademark Office requires that services be performed for *others* and that the services be real, so that internal services, for example, are not legitimate. Also, the service cannot be performed in conjunction with the applicant's larger business. For example, if the primary activity is selling goods under the mark in a grocery store, bagging groceries is not considered a separate service. Offering services only to existing shareholders is not considered providing services for others.[6] However, a service is not precluded because it is only performed for a limited segment of the public.[7]

INTERCHANGEABILITY OF PRODUCTS AND SERVICES

Service marks and trademarks are considered interchangeable for related products and services. For example, use of BIG BOB's as a mark for restaurant services would preclude the registration by a third party of BIG BOB as a trademark for hamburgers. As a corollary, if you sell BIG BOB hamburgers, you should be able to register BIG BOB as a service mark.

---

[6] Where things sometimes get tricky is where a parent offers services to a subsidiary (100 % owned) or affiliate (usually defined as at least 50% but less than 100% owned). Or what if service is provided to a joint venture?

[7] Offering services to employees and retirees has been found to constitute a service.

TYPES AND STYLES OF TRADEMARKS

Colored Marks

Any trademark or service mark can be used in color. If a mark or design is in color, it is usually registrable in black and white, in color or both. By not claiming color, the registrant is protected regardless of the color used in the mark. However, if color is an important feature of the mark, the registrant should file in color and claim the feature.[8] Optimum protection can be obtained by filing cases both in color and black and white.[9]

Compound Marks

A compound mark is usually composed of a word mark and a design element. Which part is registered as the trademark? The overall trademark, while appearing to be the most comprehensive version, is actually the most limiting, since all elements have to be infringed. Nevertheless, the overall composite mark (words plus design) can be registered.[10]

The words, if distinctive, are generally considered to make a separate impression on the purchaser and can be registered separately from the remainder of the mark. Whether the design makes a separate impression on the purchaser depends on the appearance of the design, and whether it is sufficiently distinctive to be a trademark.

Foreign Equivalents

Trademarks can be filed in English or in foreign languages. Under the Rule of Foreign Equivalents, foreign words are trans-

---

[8] Color is shown in the trademark application by lined drawings. When claiming color, the registrant should have special drawings prepared, and all supporting proofs have to be in color.

[9] A colored proof of use will support both cases.

[10] Some register the overall combination in order to protect the form of the mark actually being used as a means of pursuing counterfeiters. The more elements a mark which is being copied has, the easier it is to prove bad faith and conscious copying.

lated into English and tested for descriptiveness.[11] The examiner will require the registrant to translate any foreign words in its mark, and this information will appear on the registration certificate.

Fragrances

The Trademark Office has permitted the registration of a mark consisting of a fragrance applied to goods.[12] However, registration of fragrances per se have not been approved.

Misspellings

Frequently, a trademark is used with misspellings and abbreviations in an attempt to distinguish it over a reference or make it appear less descriptive. Sometimes this works, and sometimes it does not.[13] Misspellings are usually difficult for the public to remember.

Personal Names

Although surnames are not registrable, personal names, i.e., a combination of the first and second names, are registrable upon proof of secondary meaning. Similarly, a first name can be registered upon proof of secondary meaning. In order to register an individual's name as a trademark, it must be shown that the name functions to indicate source of origin.[14]

Slogans

Slogans are combinations of words just like any other multiple word trademark. However, if the slogan is too wordy, it

---

[11] For example, TOYOTA is a Japanese mark we are all familiar with. Some registrations for TOYOTA include the English translation, RICHFIELD, which is not descriptive of the goods.

[12] *In re Clarke*, 17 USPQ2d 1238 (TTAB 1990)

[13] Ultimately, one has to look at the particular word in relation to the goods and services being claimed and determine if a small change in the spelling will make any difference.

[14] Consent by the individual to registration is required.

will likely not be considered a trademark. It helps in registrability if the slogan has some play on words and does not make a functional statement. Descriptive terms in the slogan will normally have to be disclaimed.

Stylized Marks

If the trademark has stylized letters, does one file in typed letters, or in the stylized form? Filing in typed drawing form affords the broadest form of protection, since it is considered to cover all stylized forms. However, if the references are close, some applicants feel that they have a better chance to register if the stylized version is used.[15]

Sounds

There is nothing to prevent sounds from being registered, and they have been registered in the past, e.g., the NBC chimes. Recordings are submitted for registration. Marks can be tones with or without words, or words accompanied with music. A drawing is not required. However, the mark (sound) should be precisely described. Audio cassettes are accepted as specimens.

Titles to Programs

Titles to radio or TV programs can be registered as entertainment or for educational services. However, the programs have to be ongoing or part of a series, since single program titles are not service marks.

Titles to Periodicals

Titles to periodicals and other series of books can be registered as newsletters or magazines for certain subjects. However, titles to individual books are not registrable, since the titles are considered to be descriptive of the books.[16]

---

[15] Proofs of use of the stylized form will support both the stylized form and the typed drawing form.

[16] On this basis, names of stadiums or buildings may also be unregistrable.

Three-Dimensional Marks

The configuration of a building is registrable, if it is used in a way that could be perceived as a trademark, e.g., on a menu, stationery, etc. The three-dimensional aspect should be apparent from the proof of use and drawing and can be further brought out in the written description.[17]

House Marks

A "house mark" is a mark or logo used by a company on a wide range of products, usually in instances where it has other special trademarks. Often an examiner will allow a wider range of products for house marks than otherwise possible. An example of a statement of goods is "A house mark for chemicals for industrial use." If the applicant can provide proofs of use of several chemical product types, a sweeping statement like this may be obtained.[18]

Multiple Ownership

If the same trademark is registered by multiple parties for various goods and services, each party has a relatively narrow field of protection, and there is usually room for another.[19] Even though this mark may be used without risking infringement,

---

[17] Since buildings are now copyrighted, this form of trademark protection is less important.

[18] If the house mark designated had not been concluded, the applicant probably would have been restricted to the particular chemical products being sold, and likely, these would have been use restricted.

[19] As an example, MILLENNIUM, MILLENNIA, and misspellings thereof, are registered by numerous parties for all kinds of goods and services. In this situation, each party's exclusivity works against and limits the others, and since the public does not associate MILLENNIUM with any single source, there is room for someone else to squeeze in if a product can be found which has not been claimed.

this kind of arena is not desirable, since any enforcement rights against others will be curtailed.[20]

CROSS REFERENCES

See Chapter Two on exclusions from trademarks; Chapter Four on name selection; and Chapters Five and Six on filing. The addendum to this chapter lists examples of trademarks and service marks.

---

[20] Under these circumstances, it may be better to use a generic term and forget about filing for a trademark.

ADDENDUM ONE: TRADEMARK SCAVENGER HUNT

Forget technicalities for a moment, and let's go on a trademark scavenger hunt. Trademarks are everywhere. Want some examples? Look in the newspapers or magazines. Marks appear on every page.

Another good place to look is in the kitchen cabinets. In a quick search, the author found the following items:

1) On a package of insulation in the garage was "OWENS CORNING" in logo form and in block letters representing housemarks of Owens Corning Fiberglas Corporation; the mark "FIBERGLAS"; a statement that the "color pink" is registered; and the "PINK PANTHER" design, which was licensed by United Artists.

2) On a box of "MINUTE RICE," is the Kraft logo; "MINUTE RICE" brand in logo form; "MINUTE" in block letters; and "RICE-IPIES" for recipes on the back on the box. The company is "KRAFT GENERAL FOODS, INC." The trade name and trademarks are clearly distinguishable.

3) On a box of "SNACKWELL" crackers, in addition to the "SNACKWELL" mark, are the Nabisco logo and NABISCO FOODS name, which serve as house marks. The company name is Nabisco Foods, Inc. so that "NABISCO FOODS" is also a trade name. "TASTES SO GREAT . . . YOU'LL NEVER MISS THE FAT!" while not claimed as a trademark, is one nevertheless. This is an example of a slogan used as a trademark.

4) On a box of TABASCO sauce, "TABASCO" is shown as a federally registered trademark. Also, there is a picture of the bottle with a "Circle R." This is an example of the configuration of a container being registered. The owner company is "McILHENNY CO."

For a ready made listing of services, look in your Yellow Pages. Services range from auto repair to escort services; from legal services to publishing; from photography to real estate services; etc. Particular examples of services that the author noted follow:

1) Accountants, e.g., "A-1 Accounting" and "Abacus Accounting." You can count on an "A-1" something in every town. Think they are connected? I don't. Could this be registered? Probably not. Is "Abacus" descriptive or misdescriptive? My guess

is that it is suggestive. Most accounting firms, like law firms, have lists of surnames as their business names. They would be registrable if used as service marks, but unless they are national firms, there is little point in it. A common name like SMITH & SMITH, however, should be registered, since similar names are likely to exist elsewhere and someone else is likely to do it if you do not.

2) Air Conditioning Contractors, e.g., April Air, Axon, Better Air Conditioning, Randy's AC and Heating Service, and Total Air and Heat. "APRIL" is suggestive, has a nice touch and is easy to remember. "AXON" is arbitrary and makes the best mark. "BETTER AIR" is laudatory and weak. "TOTAL AIR" is borderline descriptive/ suggestive. "RANDY'S" is a given name and is registrable.

3) Banks, e.g., Bank of America, Compass Bank, First City Texas, NationsBank, and Security Bank. "BANK OF AMERICA" has become a strong mark through secondary meaning, and its "BA" logo is a registered service mark as well. "COMPASS" is arbitrary for banking services and makes a good trademark. A consumer will presume that all "FIRST CITY TEXAS BANKS" emanate from one source, but wonder about "FIRST CITY BANK" where Texas is not included. "NATIONSBANK" and "SECURITY BANK" are acceptable as marks; however, "security" borders on being descriptive.

4) Beauty Shops, e.g., Hair Flair Design Studio, Supercuts, Technique 2000, and Unique Hair Designs. "HAIR FLAIR" makes a good mark and has a nice play on words. "SUPERCUTS" has become strong through secondary meaning. "TECHNIQUE 2000" is arbitrary. "UNIQUE" is laudatory and weak. Most beauty shops seem to have peoples' first names which are fine for local use, but make difficult national trademarks.

Four

Selecting a Name or Mark

Many factors enter into selecting a trade name, trademark or service mark. Good names are there, waiting to be found 'and adopted. But what usually happens is that second-rate, highly descriptive names, which make poor trademarks, are chosen, because they are more apparent. Frequently, the only clearance which is done is to check a name with the secretary of state where the company is going to incorporate, which is no clearance at all.[1] The most critical place to check is the federal trademark registry, and typically that is not even considered.

Name screening and selection is an area where seeking expert assistance is justified. There are experts who can compile a list of names tailored for a particular business and who will have the proper searches performed. More importantly, these experts can assist in interpreting the search reports and accurately weigh the risks in choosing a name because they have done so hundreds of times. Identifying the "right" name or mark is equally challenging.[2]

Even if a comprehensive outside search has been conducted, and the name or mark appears clear, there is no assurance that remote users still do not exist. Frequently, the parties whom you would expect to object, don't, while those whom you never knew about are the ones that surface.[3] To further complicate matters,

---

[1] A corporate name clearance only tells you if a name can be used. It does not provide any information about whether you may be infringing another party's name or mark.

[2] There are a number of name companies that specialize in generating names for companies and products. These companies and the services they offer are fairly competitive, and the reader should shop around.

[3] Only if a prior user files a trademark application, either state or federal, or incorporates or does national advertising, can the user's name or mark be found on a search.

all it takes is one single prior local user anywhere in the U.S. to defeat a federal trademark registration.

For example, assume that a restaurant owner selects "MUNCH n'NET" as the name of his chain of sandwich shops which gives patrons access to the Internet while they eat. The owner performed a comprehensive search before adopting the mark. The proposed name was cleared, and an intent to use application was filed. After a number of stores open, a friend on a camping trip discovers a party operating a restaurant and fishing pond under the name NET AND MUNCH. From a trademark perspective, the marks, although reversed in word order, would be confusingly similar. The party who filed the intent to use application has two options: to buy name rights from the party or to lay low until his registration becomes incontestable.

In applying for trademark protection, the applicant's mark will be categorized into one of four categories: generic, descriptive, suggestive or arbitrary. The following sections discuss each of these categories and their effects on registration. Trade names are discussed separately because of their special considerations and search problems.

GENERIC MARKS

Generic marks lie on the unprotectable end of the trademark spectrum. Trademarks which are generic of the claimed goods or services *cannot be trademarks* and can be attacked, even if they are incontestable.[4] However, generic names make interesting subjects for trademarks for *unrelated* goods and services. For example, while aspirin is generic for a form of pain reliever, it is not generic for use on bicycles or kites.

DESCRIPTIVE MARKS

Descriptive marks are next on the trademark protection spectrum, and they are only protectable to a certain degree and under certain circumstances. Marks which are descriptive of the

---

[4] Like diseases in elderly humans, genericness seems to stalk mature trademarks. Cellophane and escalator are examples of marks which have become generic.

goods and services cannot be registered on the Principal Register without proof of secondary meaning, but are permitted on the Supplemental Register. Descriptive names generally make good short-term trademarks, since there is immediate public perception of the product.[5]

SUGGESTIVE MARKS

Suggestive marks are essentially mid-way on the spectrum. These are marks which suggest something about the product, but do not go so far as to be descriptive. Suggestive marks can be filed on the Principal Register.[6]

SHE THINKS I'M PRETTY

Suppose you are charged with developing the name for a new line of ties to be sold in women's boutiques. Someone proposes "I Like Your Tie." This probably would be considered descriptive so you rule it out. Same for "Great Tie," and also, it's laudatory. "She Thinks I'm Pretty" is proposed. Not bad, you say. This would likely be considered suggestive. Go for it.

ARBITRARY MARKS

Arbitrary marks offer the strongest protection of all the categories. Arbitrary marks have no resemblance or apparent relationship between the trademark and the product.[7] Over the long haul, they make the best trademarks. "KODAK," "EXXON" and "XEROX" are well-known examples of arbitrary or coined marks.

---

[5] An example of a descriptive mark that made it as a registration is "HONEY-BAKED HAM" for ham.

[6] Examples include "WHIRLPOOL" for washers, and "COPPERTONE" for tanning lotion.

[7] For example, an arbitrary mark is "APPLE" for computers. It is arbitrary because apples have nothing to do with computers.

TRADE NAMES

Trade and business names develop common law unfair competition rights the same as trademarks. Common law rights, whether trademark or trade name based, result from goodwill generated through use. Being use-based, common law rights are territorial and limited to the lines of actual business of the company.

State recordal of a trade name, although a requirement when doing business in a state, usually does not provide much protection, or expand the common law rights. Corporate recordals usually only protect against use of the exact name, so there is not much of a protective shield.

Even though trade names are precluded from registration under the Lanham Act, they may be references against marks, and trade name protection is available under Section 43(a), if another party uses a name or mark which will result in a false designation of origin (see Chapter 16). Owners who have used their trade names for at least six months can register with the U.S. Customs Service, which provides some protection against infringing imports bearing the name.

The trademark prohibition against trade names notwithstanding, protection for a trade name can be obtained indirectly by federal trademark and service mark registration. If the products being sold are limited in type and the services are well-defined, a trademark or service mark can usually be improvised.[8]

Where one runs into difficulty is when a company has a wide range of products or services. It is difficult to classify all aspects of a business under the International classification system and provide necessary proofs of use to support each trademark registration.[9] There are also cases where a company's trade name will not make a good trademark because it is a surname, is descriptive, etc. Under these circumstances, it may be a good idea

---

[8] A business can usually be defined in terms of one or more service marks. It is just a matter of thinking about it. That, and being able to provide proof of use down the road.

[9] It is important to register the key products or services. This strategy will at least offer better protection than if no products or services were registered.

to couple the name with a logo and register the combination. This will get the name before the public the same as if the trade name had been filed separately, since on a database all a searcher will see is the name and the word "design."

SEARCHING TRADEMARKS AND SERVICE MARKS

Trademarks and service marks are considerably easier to search than trade names, since the search is generally limited to products of a certain type, or services in a defined field, and state recordals are unnecessary. The Principal Register is a good place to begin to search for possibly conflicting names. It is important to file intent to use applications on the Principal Register as soon as possible to establish priority dates to the name or names. Trademarks and service marks can be searched fairly effectively by using computer databases. Most searches involve looking for confusingly similar valid registrations, or pending applications with an earlier priority date for the same or similar goods or services.[10]

For some companies, an initial screening in the library of *The Trademark Register* may be sufficient.[11] However, if a company is preparing to invest a significant amount of money in a project, it is advisable to conduct a professional, and more intensive, search. Even most outside searches performed by professionals will be at least *two months* out of date due to the lagtime in processing in the Patent and Trademark Office. Thus, it often becomes a race as to which company files a particular name first and receives the priority filing date for that name.

Good searching and an practical experience-based interpretation of the search results are critical for selecting trademarks. Sometimes, a search reveals a direct "hit" for a proposed name. If that is the case, quite simply the search is over. Otherwise, the search must continue until due diligence is established. If you dig deep enough, there will always be problems of some sort,

---

[10] If the name being searched is arbitrary, you may be able to search without limiting classes. Otherwise, you will likely have to limit the search to the class or classes of interest.

[11] This booklet is published by the Trademark Office and portions are included in the Appendices. It has a listing of depository libraries for trademarks. These offer CD ROM searching capabilities.

and some risk taking is essential or you will never be able to adopt any name.

NAME OR MARK SELECTION PROCEDURE

There are many steps involved in selecting and protecting a trade name or trademark. The following is a list of steps to consider:

1. Study the company and its business plans and products.
2. Identify the product or service and determine the special features and market.
3. Prepare a search strategy.
4. Generate a large number of names as a working list.
5. Conduct an initial screening search.
6. Screen the names in relation to one another and the products and services.
7. Select a short list of name choices.
8. Perform a comprehensive name search.
9. Initiate test marketing.
10. Make a linguistic analysis.
11. File protective trademark applications.
12. Monitor the examination process.
13. Publish the names for opposition.
14. Obtain a Notice of Allowance.
15. Select the final name.
16. Market the product or services.
17. Provide proof of use.
18. Keep track of when the registration issues.

Depending on the situation, some of the above steps can be skipped. At times other steps may be appropriate, and sometimes there are loopbacks. Businesses which are multi-faceted and have nationwide operations are the most difficult to handle, since there are more fields of business and more states to clear. Single product trademarks and service marks are the easiest to search.

SEARCHING NAMES AND MARKS

Consider the scenario where a company executive decides he wants to use "the Rose Factory" as a dba for his company, which provides mail order roses. In choosing a trade name, rule one is to clear the name to protect against unknowingly infringing an already established name. Federal rights control and the executive needs to make sure that no federal registrations or applications exist that are confusingly similar to the prospective name. Also, it is important to search for state trademarks where the company will be doing business and the corporate name registry. How would the executive go about doing the trademark searches? He would search under "rose" and "factory," as well as "Rosefactory." He would also look to see if "rose" is used with any names that could be substituted for "factory," e.g., shop, store, company, firm, etc. Should the executive look at "Flower" in combination with "Factory"? Absolutely. Searching is never finished unless the search reveals a dead ringer or eliminates all reasonable possibilities.

Let's say your represent an entrepreneur who wants to market "Future Town" remote-controlled toy robots. Where and what do you search? The first step is to search "future" and "town" on the principal register. This could be restricted to International Classes 9 (electrical devices) and 28 (toys). The run-on word "futuretown" should be searched. Probably it would also be good to look at variations such as "robot town" and "robot city." If the name still has not been precluded, then you may want to search the state trademarks in the states where the product will be marketed. Finally, you may want to look at "robot" for goods and services to see what kinds of marks exist for toy robots. The only time you can be satisfied with a search is if you get a direct hit. Otherwise, searching is open-ended.

To put things into proper perspective, *searching is everything.* It is comparable to a doctor checking blood pressure, temperature and pulse. It is impossible to determine the status of a trademark without seeing what other marks are out there. How does one conduct a search? There are various database services. Online searching is now possible in the U.S., Canada and various European countries. Technological advances make it possible to conduct searches in fifteen minutes that would have taken weeks ten years ago. There are libraries that are federal trademark depositories (see Appendix Fifteen) which provide searches on CD ROM. There are also trademark reference works in most libraries, and those proficient in searching the World

Wide Web can pursue that angle. Whatever method, it is important to conduct the most thorough search possible. In this regard, it may be advisable to hire a professional search firm or an attorney who knows trademarks to conduct and interpret the search.

Searching a company name gets more complicated, since the name must be cleared in the state of incorporation, as well as in the states where the company will do business. This means someone will have to contact the secretaries of state, which usually can be done by phone, but sometimes requires a writing a letter and a payment.[12]

Clearing a name nationwide is extremely difficult. It usually involves calling each of the individual secretaries of state. To make matters worse, a few states will no longer provide clearances over the phone, and others now require payment of fees.[13] The alternative is to use a company that sets up corporations and acts as registered agents.[14] One such organization is CT Corporation. A list of Secretary of State Offices and phone numbers is included in the Addendum to Chapter Fourteen.

PROTECT NAMES WITH INTENT TO USE

With *intent to use* (ITU) applications, the applicant has flexibility to protect trade names which never existed before. Concurrently with or preferably before incorporating, the applicant can file an ITU case on the name claiming a general statement of services. This can be restricted to more specific services during prosecution. In the meantime, statutory notice of the claim to the name has been made throughout the U.S. And if an infringer tries to use the name, the applicant will have priority rights, assuming the mark is in use and the applicant has obtained a registration.

---

[12] Sometimes, approval will be conditioned on getting a consent from another party.

[13] To obtain rights to a name nationwide, it is advisable to devise an arbitrary or coined name. In selecting a name, companies should also consider what stock symbol or ".com" prefix they will use.

[14] For screening, a short list of key states is recommended, e.g., the state of incorporation, Delaware, Texas, New York, and key market states. This will act as a barometer.

LOGOS

Logos are symbols or devices which can be corporate symbols and can be registered as trademarks or service marks. In many ways, they operate in the same way as word marks. If a word mark and a symbol are used together as a logogram, either the overall combination, or the logo (if it makes a separate impression) can be registered.

Designing logos is difficult and searching them is even more so, since design searching with a computer is difficult and manual search depositories usually is not reliable. Search firms offer design searches, but the results are usually poor and the searches are costly.

TRADE DRESS

Trade dress encompasses designs or decor which are not trademarked. That does not mean that these elements cannot be registered, although in most cases they are not. To obtain a registration, the design must be inherently distinctive or have secondary meaning.[15] Searching for conflicting trade dress makes trade name searching look easy. The only way to do this is to actually visit competitors in the proposed marketing territory and see what they are doing. This is, needless to say, a very time-consuming procedure and may actually work against you should a matter ever come before the courts.

COPYRIGHT CONSIDERATIONS

Because of a recent amendment to the Copyright Act — the Berne Convention Implementation Act — companies desiring a new image should consider the copyrightability of their designs and logos. By avoiding simple graphic designs and adopting designs with more "curly q's," logos can be created which have

---

[15] There's an ongoing argument about whether trade dress can be inherently distinctive and registrable without secondary meaning. Logically, if the trade dress is distinctive, it should be registrable, since whether it is called "trade dress" or "trademark" shouldn't make any difference (a "rose by any other name" argument.)

sufficient artistic effort to be copyrightable. Why be concerned about copyrights? Copyright protection comes practically for free and is essentially worldwide. Copyrights apply to whatever articles or services they are imprinted upon or used with. On the other hand, trademarks have to be applied for and registered class by class, country by country. Depending on the type of work, copyrights last: (1) for the life of the author plus 50 yeas; or (2) 75 years from publication, or 100 years from creation, whichever is shorter. Where international rights are needed and a design is involved, it makes sense to use copyright rights as an adjunct to trademark protection, since they are quick, cheap and offer wide coverage.

CROSS REFERENCES

Chapters Five, Six and Seven explain how to prepare, file and prosecute trademark applications.

Five

Use or Intent to Use

Applicants for trademark registration have the option to file with the U.S. Patent and Trademark Office based on use or intent to use. Until recently, filing a use-based application was the only procedure available to U.S. applicants. Under the intent to use procedure, the applicant can now reserve a trademark and receive a priority date, deferring actual use until after notice of allowance. This enables an applicant to obtain vested trademark rights before marketing products or providing services. Filing is constructive use and pre-empts the entire U.S. for the claimed products and services as of the application date.

THE OLD METHOD OF TRADEMARK FILING

The traditional way to obtain federal trademark protection in the U.S. was to sell the product in interstate commerce in the normal course of business and then apply for a federal trademark by filing a use-based application. Nine to eighteen months later the applicant would know if the mark was going to be approved for publication, and in another six months the applicant would find out if the mark was going to be opposed.

Following this procedure, it could be two years or longer before the trademark registration issues. And while the effective date of a trademark filed after November 16, 1989 is backdated to application date, applications filed before this date became effective on their issue or registration dates.

Under this antiquated system, the horse (the use) had to pull the buggy (the trademark) across a state line in order to apply for a trademark. Since use in commerce was a prerequisite to applying for a trademark, protection could not be obtained in advance. And since a trademark did not become effective until registration, there was a gap of several years where encroachers were free to move in.

Historically, trademark registrations were not that important. Trade name rights were usually left to be protected at common law, and advertising slogans traditionally were not protected.[1] This system may have worked 30 or 40 years ago, but now, this kind of lag time in acquiring rights is impractical.

Trademarks needed to be upgraded to keep pace with society, and finally, Congress responded with Trademark Act of 1988.[2] This put trademarks back on the fast track and made registration a viable business mechanism. Now, there is a better way to protect trademarks.

THE INTENT TO USE OPTION

Trademarks, service marks, trade names, advertising slogans, titles, character names, names of musical groups, etc., can be reserved and protected *before* disclosure to the public or use by filing intent to use (ITU) applications.[3] The date of filing is a priority or reference date against third parties for the claimed goods and services.[4] Under this scenario, the trademark has become the horse and is free to go forward on its own, unhindered by the buggy (the use).

USE IN COMMERCE

The Lanham Act is based on the commerce clause. Therefore, in upgrading the law, Congress could not provide independent self-executing laws or registration systems as with patents and copyrights. Rights to trademarks had to depend on use in commerce as a prerequisite.

"Use in commerce" is defined as: "the bona fide use of a mark in the ordinary course of trade, and not being made merely to preserve a right . . . ."[5] Use in commerce is an essential part of the

---

[1] There was little point in applying for a service mark on an advertising slogan that would have been used and discarded before the registration issued.

[2] Trademark Revision Act of Nov. 16, 1988.

[3] The U.S. is a latecomer to intent to use. Canada has long used a similar system where proof of use is required before registration.

[4] §7(c). The filing date is constructive use for both use-based applications and intent to use applications which result in registrations.

[5] §45

intent to use system — only proof of use is deferred. It is necessary that a trademark be used in commerce in connection with the claimed goods and services before a registration will be issued. However, proof of use was shifted from being a prerequisite for filing to being a condition for registration. And since the application establishes priority, delay due to prosecution — which used to be such a killer — is unimportant.

Under the intent to use system, which became effective November 16, 1989, procedures were established to protect a name or trademark before public disclosure or use. Upon filing with the U.S. Patent and Trademark Office on the Principal Register, a priority date is obtained to the trademark or service mark throughout the U.S. [6]

THE IMPORTANCE OF FILING EARLY

Under the Lanham Act, as originally passed, trademarks did not become effective until they were registered. The registration date was the priority date. Now whether the applicant files intent to use or use-based, *the filing date* is the priority date. This is a big, big change and the moral is clear: file fast and first.

The key to intent to use (ITU) filings is when the commerce clause is triggered. The Trademark Act of 1988 allows the applicant to postpone or delay the commerce requirement until *after* the notice of allowance for the mark has been received. Therefore, use in commerce is still required before a registration issues, which satisfies the statutory requirement. ITU's are available to large companies, individuals and entrepreneurs alike to protect or reserve trademarks prior to forming a business or developing a product.

For example, a movie studio files an intent to use service mark for entertainment services on "The Return of the Jungle Son," together with various trademark applications covering proposed merchandising items. If the movie is finished and released, proof of use is submitted to support the applications. The

---

[6] This is a big deal since previously protection depended upon territorial use.

registration, when it issues, will be effective for reference purposes on its filing date.

Proposed trademarks should be protected early-on by intent to use filings. ITU's give the applicant time to develop the product or business and to test the market. With ITU's, applicants have an option right that they can exercise if it is advantageous to do so, or walk away from if it isn't. If an applicant's mark is rejected, he or she can abandon it. If it is registrable and the market conditions are right, then the applicant can proceed accordingly with his or her business plan. Consequently, applicants can "hedge their bets" by filing. Filing ITU's should be standard procedure, a no-brainer; yet most managers seem to overlook this option.

The 1988 Revision of the Trademark Act did not receive much publicity in the business world at the time of passage, which is perhaps why its significance is only now starting to be appreciated. ITU filings are considered by many to represent the most significant change in trademarks since the Lanham Act in 1946. And the fact that over fifty percent of all filings are now intent to use supports this claim.

THE ACTUAL USE ALTERNATIVE

Under the Lanham Act, as revised in 1988, filings still can be made based on actual use. This gives the applicant a filing choice. However, filing an actual use application requires certain additional information over and above an intent to use application. Proofs (specimens) and dates of first use have to be provided and the particular products or services used in commerce have to be specified. Other products cannot be added later on.[7] If the company shown on the proofs of use is different from the applicant, the examiner will inquire as to how they are associated. If the company is a subsidiary, use is considered to inure to the parent. Otherwise, a copy of the supporting license is required so that quality control will be apparent.[8]

---

[7] There is no provision, as there is in Canada, where the applicant can base part of its application on intent to use and part on actual use. In the U.S., the applicant has to do it one way or the other.

[8] Usually it is sufficient to disclose the quality control portions of the agreement.

If an applicant is able to satisfy all the use requirements, the actual use application should be filed. There is at least one advantage to filing this way: the extra filing fee added for intent to use applications is not applicable to use-based applications.[9]

However, if the product has not been marketed, or if the applicant is not yet certain about all the products, it is inadvisable to wait to file. It is important to file intent to use and get a priority date. Intent to use allows applicants the opportunity to protect the marks for their products and services before actual use.

ADVANTAGES OF ITU FILINGS

The primary advantages of intent to use filings over use-based trademark filings are noted below:

(1) The applicant can file sooner and get an earlier filing date. This is because an ITU application can be dispatched immediately without waiting to gather proofs of use and determine usage dates.[10]

(2) The applicant does not have to reveal any usage dates until after publication. This keeps opponents guessing about what the applicant's priority rights are until they file opposition and seek discovery.

(3) The applicant causes the examiner to do a piecemeal examination, which generally favors the applicant. With ITU's, the examiner is forced to focus separately on the classification of the goods and services and the prior references and is unable to reject the proofs of use to supplement other rejections.

(4) The applicant can wait to see if a mark will be rejected or allowed before bringing the product or service to the market. Therefore, the applicant does not have a lot of front-end market costs where the status of the mark is questionable.

(5) The applicant is able to file several applications on several different proposed marks while making a final marketing decision on which mark to use.

(6) Since intent to use is equal to actual use, the applicant does not have to wait for the sale of the trademarked product or

---

[9] Currently $100 more per class.

[10] Gathering proofs may not be a problem if the applicant is the sole proprietor, but it is a major hurdle in large corporations.

for services to be performed under the mark in interstate commerce before filing.

(7) The applicant is able to claim the goods or services broadly and not limit them until proof of use is supplied. This gives the applicant maximum leeway to develop a full product line.

(8) The applicant is better able to fend off oppositions since discovery is less burdensome and use cannot be questioned.

THE APPLICATION

Trademark applications designate the specific goods and services and indicate the class or classes of goods that the mark will be used on. No proofs of use or dates of use are required unless the applicant is filing based on use. Both types of applications require drawings. These can be formal drawings or typed letter drawings.[11]

FILING COSTS

The current filing fee for trademark applications is about two hundred dollars and fifty dollars per application per class.[12] Payment of a single fee will entitle the applicant to a filing date. The filing fee is the same whether all classes are put in a single application, or whether a series of separate applications are filed. Before the application is published for opposition, a makeup fee, based on the number of classes remaining in the application, must be paid. If filing was made on an intent to use basis, an additional fee is required upon submission of the proofs of use when the application is converted to a use-based application.[13]

TRADE NAMES

Although trade or business names cannot be trademarked per se, a trade name can be registered, *if it is used as a trademark or service mark.* Once a trade name is selected, the applicant can

---

[11] Typed drawings are the way to go to file quickly. The applicant simply types the mark in all capital letters on a sheet of paper.

[12] Currently the filing fee is $245 per class.

[13] This isn't required until after notice of allowance. Currently the proof of use fee is $100 per class.

reserve it by filing an intent to use trademark application. The trick is to define the services and products in terms of what the company does or intends to do. Federal trademarks will override any state corporate name recordals which may be made by other parties.[14]

ADVERTISING SLOGANS

Advertising slogans can be trademarks or service marks. This means that they can be registered. Why isn't this done more often? The reason used to be that the periods of projected use were usually shorter than the time for acquiring a registration. However, now with intent to use, priority rights can be established before use upon filing an application so that slogans can be protected before use.

SLOGANS TO GO

Surprisingly, most advertising agencies have not come to appreciate the opportunities that abound with intent to use filings. They can literally bank slogans or advertising themes by filing intent to use applications and have them available to license to clients. (In order to avoid the use requirement, the agency can simply refile after an application has run out of extensions.) What client wouldn't want a guaranteed available name? The service would be worth a premium.

BONA FIDE USE

To file an intent to use application, the applicant must claim a legitimate bona fide intent to use the mark, and to file based on use, the applicant has to have legitimate use in ordinary trade.[15] However, licensing can be the mechanism of use for both types of filings.

---

[14] State approval of a name is necessary to do business in the state. However, prior federal rights will control. The author has seen numerous instances where a party had to change the name of a business because there were overriding trademark rights.

[15] §45 "Use in Commerce." Therefore, token use is passé.

EQUALIZING EFFECT

Intent to use levels the playing field with foreign parties. Foreign applicants can file under Section 44(b) and get a registration without use in the U.S. if there is use in the applicant's home country. However, U.S. applicants now can obtain priority rights based on the filing date, which is significantly better than having to show use in order to file, or not having the registration effective until its issue date.

HYPOTHETICAL EXAMPLES

1. Joe conceives of a product and a trademark. The product is an inflexible, extendible dog walking leash for make-believe dogs. The idea is to market a selection of leashes representing different breeds of dogs to encourage people to exercise by walking their imaginary dogs. His trademark is MY BEST FRIEND. Joe files an ITU application and has a prototype product prepared. His application is rejected because there are other pre-existing registrations for MY BEST FRIEND for dog-related products. Joe files another ITU application for TAKE ME WALKING. This one is approved for publication. No one opposes and a notice of allowance issues. At this point, Joe is assured of getting a registration, provided he submits proof of use. Joe licenses a manufacturer who produces the product. Voila! Joe is in business.

2. Red conceives a project where he will trademark various football-related terms, e.g., QUICK KICK, TOUCHDOWN, FIRST DOWN etc., for merchandising products. Even though the words may be generic or descriptive relative to football games, he thinks that they would be trademarkable relative to various products. Red buys several reference books on football and compiles a list of potential trademarks. He then goes to the local library, which is a trademark depository, and searches the terms. He files ITU applications on five terms with the intent to license them. Several of the marks are approved by the examiner. The approved marks are published and no one opposes. Red finds a licensing agent who is interested in licensing the marks. The agent cuts a deal with a manufacturer who makes the product and provides Red with proof of use so that registrations can issue.

CROSS REFERENCES

See Chapter Six for general information on the preparation of applications. Chapter Seven covers prosecution.

Six

The Trademark Application

Federal trademark rights result from the registration of applications with the U.S. Patent and Trademark Office. Each trademark has to be processed and registered individually. This chapter discusses the requirements for preparing and filing applications with the U.S. Patent and Trademark Office.

PROCEDURE

Trademarks must be obtained one by one.[1] Preparing and filing trademark applications is relatively simple, and the procedures can be easily mastered. Owners can file and prosecute their own applications, or be represented by an attorney.[2] If an attorney is going to file the application, he or she does not need to be a registered patent attorney, since any attorney is authorized to practice before the Trademark Office.[3] However, the owner cannot use a patent agent, since patent agents are not permitted to handle trademarks. The Patent and Trademark Office will not assist in the selection of attorneys.

---

[1] Perhaps one day a company will be able to submit a blanket registration for all its trademarks and have them examined and registered as a package. This would greatly ease the burden on the Patent and Trademark Office. Trademark rights exist collectively at common law, and all the company would need to do to be compatible with the Constitution is confirm use in commerce.

[2] The Trademark Office says its application form can be completed in 15 minutes and that's probably not far off for the second or third times. Of course, completion of any form requires that the information be at hand.

[3] An attorney has to be specifically licensed to handle patents, but there is no equivalent requirement for trademarks. While any attorney is authorized to file trademarks, there is a big difference in being permitted to do something and knowing how to do it.

Correspondence from the Trademark Office will be sent to the applicant, unless there is an attorney of record, in which case all correspondence will be with the attorney. If the applicant is not domiciled in the U.S., an agent to receive service must be designated in writing and correspondence will be held with the designated agent unless there is an attorney. Duplicate correspondence will not be sent. A change of address can be designated in writing.

THE APPLICANT

The trademark owner must apply for a federal trademark. Therefore, neither a licensee nor an attorney, nor someone given a power of attorney, can sign the application papers. An officer should sign for a corporation or an association.[4] Only one partner is required to sign for a partnership. However, all joint venture partners should sign.

> **VERIFICATION**
>
> Trademark applications and other documents must be verified. This means that the statements have to be executed before a notary public or that the prescribed declaration be used. Using declarations is easier, since you can execute the declaration anywhere, anytime and don't have to be concerned about whether the notary acted properly and was legally authorized.
> Declarations are authorized by Rule 2.20 for use in lieu of any oath, affidavit, verification or sworn statement prescribed for by the Rules.

Normally, trademark applications are verified by declarations rather than affidavits. A declaration is a form of self-notarization under threat of statutory sanctions where the applicant or officer or member of the corporation or association confirms that: "all statements made of his or her own knowledge are true and that all statements filed on information and belief are believed to be true."

---

[4] This duty cannot be delegated by granting another party a power of attorney.

On the same paper the declarant must be warned that: "willful false statements and the like are punishable by fine or imprisonment, or both (18 U.S.C. 1001) and may jeopardize the validity of the application or document or any registration resulting therefrom."

REQUIREMENTS OF APPLICATION

Applications must be filed in English and be on letter-size paper (81/2 by 11 inches or 21.6 v.27.9 cm.) At least a one and one-half inch (3.8 cm.) margin is required on the left-hand side and on the top.

An application has the following parts:

(1) The name of the applicant.

(2) The citizenship of the applicant. If the applicant is a corporation, the state or nation under which the corporation is organized is required. For partnerships, the name and citizenship of each general partner is required.

(3) The domicile and post office address of the applicant.

(4) Whether the applicant is applying under Section 1(a) or 1(b) of the Act. The former requires that the applicant have adopted and is using the mark, shown in the accompanying drawing, and the latter requires that the applicant have a bona fide intent to use the mark, shown in the accompanying drawing, in commerce.[5]

(5) If the application is made under Section 1(a) of the Act, the particular goods or services on or in connection with which the mark is used must be specified. If application is made under Section 1(b), the particular goods or services with which the applicant has a *bona fide intent to use* the mark shall be specified.[6]

(6) The goods or services according to the official classification. (See the Classification Index, Appendix One.) If the applicant does not know the classes or states them incorrectly, the examiner will correct the classification.

---

[5] There is also a provision for applying under Section 44 of the Act which allows foreign nationals to register.

[6] If a foreign national is filing based on treaty rights, the statement of goods or services cannot exceed the scope of the goods or services covered by the foreign application or registration.

(7) If the application is under Section 1(a), it must state the date of applicant's first use as a trademark or service mark on or in connection with the goods or services specified in the application, and the date of the applicant's first use in commerce regarding same, specifying the nature of such commerce, i.e., whether interstate or foreign commerce.[7]

(8) If a Section 1(a) application is filed, the mode, manner or method of affixing, applying or otherwise using the mark on or in connection with the goods or services must be specified. In an application under Section 1(b), the *intended* mode, manner or method of applying, affixing or otherwise using the mark on or in connection with the goods or services is required.

(9) An application under Section 1(a) must include averments to the effect:

> that the applicant is believed to be the owner of the mark sought to be registered; that the mark is in use in commerce, specifying the nature of the commerce; that no other entity to the best of the declarant's knowledge and belief, has the right to use such mark in commerce, either in the identical form or in such near resemblances as to be likely, when applied to the goods or services of such other entity, to cause confusion, or to cause mistake, or to deceive; that the specimens or facsimiles show the mark as used on or in connection with the goods or services; and that the facts set forth in the application are true.

(10) An application under Section 1(b) must include averments to the effect:

> that the applicant believes himself or herself, or the firm, corporation or association in whose behalf he or she makes the verification, to be entitled to use the mark in commerce, and that no other person, firm, corporation or association, to the best of his or her knowledge and

---

[7] Dates of use are required for goods or services in each class. Where more than one item of goods or services is specified, the dates of use need only be for one of the items, provided that is specified.

belief, has the right to use such mark in commerce either in an identical form of the mark or in such near resemblance to the mark as to be likely, when used on or in connection with the goods of such other person, to cause confusion, or to cause mistake, or to deceive; and that the facts set forth in the application are true.

An applicant is not permitted to file under both Sections 1(a) and 1(b) in a single application, or amend a use-based application to an intent to use application.[8]

An application may be filed in a single class or multiple classes; provided the goods or services are *specifically identified*, and the applicant has either used the mark on all of the specified goods or services, or has a bona fide intention to do so.[9] Filing intent to use has the advantage of allowing the applicant to generalize the scope of goods.

An application can be divided into two or more separate applications upon written request after filing. Therefore, if one class is delayed in prosecution, the other classes can be moved to a separate application so that they proceed to registration.

Care is required to avoid charges of false statements or fraud in the application which could result in the registration being found to be unenforceable. Many applications filed with the U.S. Patent and Trademark Office are prepared carelessly and have mistakes, and applications that are assembled in good form and are mistake-free generally receive better consideration.

---

[8] In Canada, a single case can be use-based and intent to use.

[9] In most foreign countries, the applicant can file for all the goods or services in a class without use. In the U.S., the applicant has to have use for each item in the claim. This item-by-item use requirement is unduly strict and discriminates against U.S. trademark owners. Foreigners can convention file in the U.S. and preempt entire classes, while the U.S. applicant is hobbled by the specific use requirement. Conversely, if a U.S. registrant is filing abroad, he or she would be limited to the particular goods where there was actual use. Because of this restriction, there aren't many U.S. applications that are convention filed. The U.S. priority is abandoned in order to increase the scope of coverage of the goods or services.

PRINCIPAL VS. SUPPLEMENTAL REGISTER

There are two federal registers: the Principal Register which is the one where applicants want their marks to go, and the Supplemental Register. The Principal Register provides the applicant-registrant with a number of special rights. The advantages of having a mark included on the Principal Register are:

(1) The applicant is entitled to a constructive use date as of the date of filing throughout the U.S.

(2) A registration is constructive notice of the claim of ownership so as to eliminate any defense of good faith adoption and use after the date of registration.

(3) A registration may become incontestable from certain attacks.

(4) Registration is prima facie evidence of validity of the registered mark, of registration of the mark and of the registrant's ownership and exclusive right to use the mark.

(5) Registration may be used to bar importation of trademarked products into the U.S.

Although registrations on the Supplemental Register cost the same as registrations on the Principal Register, registrants do not get nearly as much in the way of rights. Registrants can bring suit in Federal Court and are able to use the "Circle R" notation. Furthermore, the Trademark Office can cite a registration on the Supplemental Register as a reference, but otherwise the registrant gains little over common law rights.[10] There is no preemption of territory, constructive use, incontestability, or presumptions of validity, or of exclusive right to use, and supplemental registrations cannot be recorded with Customs.

Why then are supplemental registrations used? For the same reason they have always existed. There is some benefit in using supplemental registrations to obtain rights abroad for configurations of containers and packages. And since the supplemental register is there, it has utility for other situations.

---

[10] The owner could probably get into Federal Court anyway based on false designation of origin under Section 43(a).

If a trademark cannot be registered on the Principal Register, some applicants will obtain a Supplemental Registration.[11] Most often, applicants will obtain a Supplemental Registration after battling with an examiner over descriptiveness. In this situation, the applicant cannot obtain a Principal Registration and will decide to take a Supplemental Registration and return to fight another day. It is good practice to always file first on the Principal Register, even if the mark is questionable. If the examiner stipulates that the mark does not belong on the Principal Register, the applicant then has the opportunity to argue the point, which may just sway the examiner.

Section 27 provides that: "Registration of a mark on the supplemental register . . . shall not preclude registration by the registrant on the principal register . . . ." It used to be that some parties felt that accepting the Supplemental Register weakened the mark. However, Section 27 took care of this by providing that "registration on the supplemental register shall not constitute an admission that the mark has not acquired distinctiveness."

Intent to use applications cannot be filed on the Supplemental Register. Therefore, before converting an ITU case from the Principal to the Supplemental Register, the applicant needs to provide proof of use. This can be done concurrently with an amendment to the Supplemental Register.

THE MARK

The applicant must decide what form the mark will take on the application. Should the application be filed using a typed drawing of the mark or a stylized form which would require a formal drawing? Should the application include descriptive terms or should they be left out? The applicant has a lot of flexibility in structuring the mark, since a stylized proof of use will support both stylized marks and typed drawing forms.

The applicant needs to consider how the mark will be used to make sure the form of the mark will be supported. With in-

---

[11] It used to be that a mark had to be used one year before an application could be filed in the Supplemental Register. This requirement was deleted in the 1988 Trademark Act.

tent to use, the applicant can conform the proofs of use to the mark as filed. *Filing in typed drawing form is the quickest and easiest and usually results in the broadest coverage.*

Other considerations in determining what form of the mark to use are the forms of the marks in the references that the applicant is trying to distinguish over and the forms of the mark, if any, which the applicant has filed on before. However, there is nothing to prevent the applicant from using the same mark again, if the goods and services are different.

If the applicant is covering the same goods or services, the mark needs to be in a different format or style. Thus, there can be cases covering the same goods which are in typed drawing form, stylized form and lined for color.[12] Similarly, the mark can be registered with a logo or without.

THE DRAWING

An essential part of the application is the drawing of the mark. A drawing is required for both use-based and intent to use applications.[13] The drawing is required despite the fact that the applicant also submits proofs of use in the same application. The drawing is the official representation of the mark. It is what the application references in order to define the mark. The application may refer to the mark elsewhere, and the mark may appear in various forms in the specimens, but the drawing shows the form of the mark actually claimed. This is what will be published in the *Official Gazette*.

The formal requirements of the drawing are as follows. The paper size is the same as the rest of the application, i.e., no oversized sheets are permitted. A good grade of bond paper is suitable. The drawing should be at least 2.5 inches high and no more than 4 inches wide and located approximately in the center of the sheet of paper. All drawings must be made by pen or by a photolithigraphic reproduction, or a printer's proof copy. Every line and letter must be black and gray — tints are not permitted. White pigment to cover lines is unacceptable. Broken lines may be used to show the placement of the mark on the

---

[12] The same proofs of use will suffice for all three cases.
[13] In certain cases a drawing is excused, e.g., for scent marks.

goods, or subject matter not claimed as part of the mark. Where color is a feature of the mark, lining is employed as shown in the official color code. (See Appendix Six.)

A typewritten heading should appear across the top of the drawing beginning one inch from the top edge and not exceeding a third of the sheet. The heading should have the applicant's name; post office address; the dates of first use of the mark and typical goods and services. Margins of at least one inch should be on the sides and bottom.

If a typed drawing is used, the mark is typed directly on the drawing sheet using capital letters. Typically bold print is used. Enlarged type is permitted, but is not essential. Drawn drawings are typically cut-out in a square or rectangle and taped to the sheet.[14]

CLASSIFICATION

In order to complete the application form and determine the costs of filing, the applicant needs to classify the goods and services. The U.S. follows the International Classification System (Appendix One) which is used by most countries.[15] This classification system sometimes is not adequate, because of changing subject matter, but it is what we are stuck with.

A separate filing fee is required for each class. However, if the applicant includes at least one filing fee with the application, the applicant will be given a filing date and debited for the remainder of the fees which are due. If the applicant has a deposit account, the additional fees will be deducted; otherwise, the applicant will be invoiced when the examiner issues the first office action.

When in doubt about how to classify, the applicant should go with the fewer number of classes and let the examiner make a classification determination. He or she has reference manuals

---

[14] Appendices Four and Five show sample drawing sheets for typed and drawn marks.

[15] The U.S. adopted the International System in 1973 and it has been adopted by about 100 countries.

available to show how other goods or services have been classified, and the applicant may be able to save a filing fee.[16]

Classification is discretionary, and the examiner has the final call. Classification is not supposed to limit or expand the applicant's rights. But searching is class-driven, and where a registrant is classified makes a difference regarding what rights third parties perceive the registrant to have.

PROOF OF USE

At any time an applicant who has filed an ITU application may amend the application to show use:

At any time during examination of an application filed under subsection (b), an applicant who has made use of the mark in commerce may claim the benefits of such use for purposes of this Act, by amending his or her application to bring it into conformity with the requirements of subsection (a). [17]

The applicant can allege use by filing an Amendment to Allege Use during the pre-publication period before, or by filing a Statement of Use after Notice of Allowance.

PROVING USE IN COMMERCE

There are three ways to prove use in commerce: (1) the applicant can make a Declaration of Use when filing a use-based application form; (2) the applicant can amend an intent to use application by filing an Amendment to Allege Use before the application goes to publication and (3) the applicant can file a Declaration of Use after notice of allowance.

When the Notice of Allowance issues, the applicant has six months during which to file the proofs of use. A second six-month extension can be obtained automatically upon payment

---

[16] A Classification Manual can be ordered from the International Trademark Association.

[17] §1(c)

of a fee. Additional extensions can be taken for good cause and upon paying additional fees. *The overall limit on extensions is 36 months from the notice of allowance.*[18]

In submitting proofs, *three* current specimens are required. These can be the same or different. Also, the dates of first use and first use in commerce must be given. If use has not taken place for all the goods which are claimed, the excess goods should be deleted from the application.

SPECIMENS

For use-based applications, the applicant must submit three specimens with the application.[19] The specimens should be duplicates of the labels, tags or containers bearing the trademark or displays associated with the goods bearing the trademark.[20] Specimens must be flat and can not exceed 81/2 inches by 11 inches. (Usually specimens will be much smaller.)

Facsimiles can be provided, e.g., copies of a photograph showing the mark when conventional specimens cannot be furnished. In submitting proofs, all can be the same or they can be different.[21]

For service marks, specimens can show uses of the mark in advertising or sale of the services. Audio tapes are permitted (usually the examiner will require a transcription of the key portions of the written record.) The author has even used photographs of television screens showing advertisements as proof.

POWER OF ATTORNEY

A power of attorney is not required, if the applicant is filing an application for himself, or as a principal for a corporation or partnership. Usually, where an attorney is involved, a power of attorney is included with the application form. If an attorney makes an appearance in a case, the examiner can request a power

---

[18] §1(d)

[19] Prior to the 1988 Act, five specimens were required.

[20] Documents associated with the goods or their sale can be submitted if specimens are not available.

[21] Although not required, if the product is new, it is helpful to provide a brochure if one is available.

of attorney, if one has not been submitted. The power can be revoked by the applicant at any time.

MISCELLANEOUS

If the mark is not readily apparent, it should be described, e.g., if the mark is in colors or it has a design, the colors and design should be described. Sample prior related registrations by the applicant should be identified. If the applicant claims use through a related company, this should be disclosed.

Preparing a trademark application is not difficult. It can usually be done without the services of an attorney, and if the applicant runs into problems later, an attorney can be engaged. Trademark application forms from the U.S. Patent and Trademark Office are found in Appendices Two and Three. The applicant simply needs to choose the applicable form and complete it according to the accompanying instructions. When submitting an application, the applicant should include a stamped self-addressed postcard, so that the Trademark Office will date stamp the serial number and filing date and return the postcard for the applicant's records.

ONLINE SERVICE

The home page of the U.S. Patent and Trademark office is www@uspto.gov. This contains information on how to prepare and file trademark applications and provides certain downloadable forms.

CROSS REFERENCES

Chapter Seven covers proof of use and prosecution.

Seven

Prosecution and Proof of Use

Filing a trademark application with the U.S. Patent and Trademark Office does not result in a trademark. The applicant is merely setting the stage for a ritual called ex parte prosecution where the applicant and the examiner at the U.S. Patent and Trademark Office argue about registrability of the trademark. The process is usually started by a rejection and ends (if the applicant wins) with a notice of allowance or acceptance of proof of use. If the examiner issues a final rejection, the applicant can either withdraw, start over or appeal.

Prosecution commences when the trademark application is filed with the U.S. Patent and Trademark Office. Initially, the application is screened for form to ensure that filing requirements are met, e.g., that the application has been signed, that it includes a drawing, that the application fee has been paid, etc. (See Chapter Six.) If the application is complete, the application is accorded a filing date, and a filing receipt is mailed to the applicant, or if an attorney has been designated, to the attorney. The application is entered on the Trademark Office's computer system, and search firms are provided access to the data.[1] Usually, there is a two-month or longer lag time between filing and when the public can access the data. This means that any trademark search is at least sixty days out of date when it is done.[2]

REVIEW BY THE EXAMINER

The examiner at the U.S. Patent and Trademark Office ex-

---

[1] Access may be granted earlier, but it should not be. If an application may subsequently be rejected as incomplete, it should never be put into a computer database where it may become a reference for or against a third party.

[2] Desirably, the applicant should do a supplemental due diligence search once the application is of record.

amines the mark for registrability and determines if the clarification is proper. In theory, an action will issue three to four months after filing; although complex cases with multiple classes take longer. Most examiners are overworked and many are new.[3] And although new examiners are monitored, there is a wide variance in results.[4]

The examiner follows one procedure for intent to use applications and another for use-based filings. Intent to use applications are examined in two stages. In the first stage, an examination is held for form and registrability. In the second stage, the goods and services are compared to the proofs of use. Use-based applications receive a complete review all at one time. Registrability of a mark often depends on what "references" the examiner finds. "References" are any prior registrations or pending applications that support or conflict with the application being examined.

WHAT ARE REFERENCES?

In determining whether a mark is registrable, trademark examiners do not consider existing state or common law trademarks or lapsed federal registrations. They only look at valid Principal and Supplemental Registrations for conflicting marks. Also, since filing dates are priority dates, the examiners are forced to consider pending applications which predate the applicant's filing date. What happens here is that the applicant is warned that his or her case may be rejected on another application (which is identified), if it becomes a registration. Prosecution is allowed to proceed as far as it can and then the application is placed in abeyance pending determination of registrability of the reference.

---

[3] Working at the Patent and Trademark Office is often a stepping stone to other jobs.

[4] Unfortunately, registrability depends in part on luck of the draw. For borderline cases, one examiner may reject the application while another may allow it.

The examiner's action will usually be dictated by what references were found on the Trademark Registers. If there are only formal matters to handle, the examiner will generally phone the applicant or the applicant's attorney and attempt to resolve the matter. Telephone calls from the examiner are usually good news for the applicant; the bad news typically arrives by mail. If an agreement is reached, the examiner will issue a confirming action.[5]

If pertinent references are found, if the examiner considers the mark descriptive, or if the examiner has another objection, a written non-final Office Action will issue, and the applicant will be given six months to respond. This is where the applicant must counter the rejection by arguing practicalities.[6] The applicant should use every possible argument, since they often have a cumulative effect.

If the application is use-based, or when proof of use is submitted in an intent to use application, the examiner may show concern if the proofs are used by a party other than the applicant. "Related parties" may use a trademark, and an applicant's statement that the company using the mark is a "wholly owned subsidiary" is usually sufficient to establish the company as a related party. If the party is unrelated or less than 100% owned, the applicant will be asked to provide proof that the applicant exercises quality control. Usually, it will be sufficient to submit copies of pertinent portions of the license which show the quality control provisions.[7] The examiner is simply seeking proof that the nature and quality of the goods is controlled.

APPLICANT'S RESPONSE

If the examiner takes exception to some part of the application, an Office Action will be issued to the applicant. There is no particular form for responding to an Office Action. The applicant needs to respond in writing, and following conventional

---

[5] No reply is necessary unless the applicant disagrees with the examiner's stipulation.

[6] A word to the wise. Don't try to argue cases using broad generalizations. Existing trademark cases can be found to support any position a party wants to take.

[7] Confidential information can be removed or blocked out.

practice, the case style, or identification, is typed on the upper left of the first page.[8] The self-adhesive label that comes with the Office Action should be placed in the upper right corner.

If the applicant is responding without amending (modifying) the application, the applicant should title the paper as a "Response." If the applicant is making changes in the application to avoid objections or correct informalities, the reply is termed an "Amendment."

A Response begins with the following language: "This is responsive to the Official Action (or Office Action) of_____." Then, the applicant responds, point by point, to the issues raised in the Office Action. An Amendment traditionally begins with the language: "Responsive to the Official Action (or Office Action) of _____, please amend the above-identified application as follows: . . . ."

In responding, the applicant should enter whatever amendments are needed. The applicant should include a "Remarks" section after the amendments which summarizes and explains the changes that were made. The applicant should address, point by point, every contention raised by the examiner in a polite, non-argumentative manner and conclude the response with the words "Respectfully Submitted" and the applicant's signature. In every amendment, the exact word or words to be stricken out or inserted in the application must be specified and the precise point indicated where the deletion or insertion shall be made. If several amendments are made in the same section, it is best to rewrite the clause.

Responding to an Office Action usually is not hard, since any trademark issue always has two sides, and the burden of proof to uphold the rejection is on the examiner.

If the rejection is based on descriptiveness, the applicant has three options: to amend the application to the Supplemental Register; to provide a statement indicating distinctiveness under Section 2(f) or to offer proof of secondary meaning.[9] In some cases, the applicant may have to argue that the mark is descrip-

---

[8] Identifying data may include the mark, serial number, filing class and name of the applicant and examining group.

[9] Descriptive marks can be placed on the Supplemental Register (SR). However, generic names cannot gain trademark status by being placed on the SR.

tive and not generic. No amount of secondary meaning can give legal protection to a generic name, so this argument must be won if the mark is going to issue at all.

If the mark has been rejected as descriptive and not been in use for five years and there is little tangible proof of secondary meaning, the applicant can file an amendment indicating the change from Principal to Supplemental Register. In the "Remarks" section, the applicant simply states that the descriptiveness rejection is moot.

Other common amendments that the applicant may have to make relate to:

- Correcting the statement of the goods or services. Anytime the applicant has a long list of goods or claim services, it is almost automatic that the examiner will find something objectionable.[10]
- Changing the identification or classification of the goods or services to add or delete classes. Usually the examiner will advise as to what should be done. If the applicant adds classes, an extra fee will be charged.
- Changing the Affidavit or Declaration. If the affidavit or declaration was defective, the applicant is given the opportunity to submit a substitute declaration properly signed and verified by the applicant.
- Amending the drawing to conform the mark to the proofs of use. The drawing can only be amended if the mark is not materially altered. To amend the drawing, the applicant will have to submit a substitute drawing.
- Correcting the designation or identity of the owner and identifying additional partners or joint venture participants.
- Providing substitute proofs of use in Section 1(a) applications. An declaration or affidavit will have to be submitted by the applicant that these were in use prior to filing the application.
- Making an amendment to allege use for Section 1(b) applications. The applicant can do this now or wait until after receiving a notice of allowance.

---

[10] The applicant can change, delete and limit but cannot add to or expand, the goods or services.

CONFIDENTIALITY OF APPLICATIONS

Patent applications are maintained confidential by the U.S. Patent and Trademark Office during prosecution. You would think the same would hold for trademark applications. Not so. Anyone can obtain copies of the file wrapper of any application at any point whether it resulted in registrations or not. This also means that anyone can get a copy of the file history. This is something to think about when the applicant is making arguments in connection with possible subsequent suits.

DISTINCTIVENESS UNDER SECTION 2(f)

A Section 2(f) Declaration confirms that the applicant has used the mark "exclusively and continuously for five years in commerce." If the applicant seeking registration can prove *five years* of substantially exclusive and continuous use in commerce of the mark, the applicant should consider claiming distinctiveness under Section 2(f). This is considered as prima facie evidence that the mark has become distinctive of the applicant's goods.[11]

SECONDARY MEANING

If the examiner finds the mark to be merely descriptive, the applicant can provide evidence to show that the trademark is distinctive and does in fact function as a trademark. The applicant should submit evidence of sales, advertising and surveys to show that the public perceives the name to be a mark and not a descriptive term. The process where a name becomes indicative of the source of the goods is called secondary meaning.

Proving secondary meaning involves establishing the (1) length and continuity of use, (2) the extent of advertising and

---

[11] It is not mandatory for the Trademark Office to accept the Sec. 2(f) Affidavit. Therefore, if the applicant can offer some forms of proofs as attachments, as opposed to making a bare bones declaration, this will generally help move things along.

promotion and (3) sales figures. In responding, the applicant must assemble a packet of supporting material and have a sales manager or marketing VP sign an affidavit that the trademark is distinctive of the claimed products or services. If the applicant filed intent to use, he will have to concurrently provide proof of use. But if the applicant has a substantial amount of evidence, the examiner usually will accept it, since the Trademark Office has neither the time nor the funds to conduct a counter survey.[12]

AMENDMENT TO ALLEGE USE

This is the procedure the applicant follows to convert an intent to use application to a use-based application.[13] There are a number of situations in which an applicant will want to convert an intent to use application to one that is use-based. For example it is necessary if the applicant has to convert to the Supplemental Register, since ITU applications are not permitted on the Supplemental Register. Another reason is that applicant may want to assign the mark and since there is a prohibition against assigning ITU cases, the solution is to convert to a use-based application, which is assignable.

An amendment to allege use provides the material that was not submitted with the original ITU application and includes:

(1) A verified statement by the applicant that: "the applicant is believed to be the owner of the mark sought to be registered and that the mark is in use in commerce, specifying the date of the applicant's first use of the mark and the first date of the use of the mark in commerce, the type of commerce, those goods or services specified in the application on or in connection with which the mark is in use in commerce and the mode or manner in which the mark is used on or in connection with the goods or services."

---

[12] It is a different deal in inter partes or infringement actions where two companies are doing battle. There will likely be surveys on both sides.

[13] §1(c)

(2) Three specimens of the mark as used in commerce.
(3) A fee (currently $100 per class.)
An amendment to allege use can only be made when the applicant has used the mark in commerce for *all* the goods or services specified in the application. Excess goods or services should be deleted by amendment. Dates of use need only be specified for one item per class.[14]

REEXAMINATION

After the applicant has submitted a response or an amendment, the examiner will reexamine the application by studying the arguments which were presented in the response and either continue and expand upon them, accept the applicant's point of view or issue a FINAL action.[15] Following a final action, an applicant has six months to either comply with the outstanding requirements or file a notice of appeal.

RESPONSE AFTER FINAL ACTION

The applicant can ask the examiner to reconsider a final rejection, but that will usually be fruitless and does not toll the six month response time.[16] At this point, the applicant's options are to comply with the examiner's demands or appeal. Often, the best course of action for the applicant is to phone the examiner to see if there is any way the application can be amended to avoid the rejection. Also, if it is a multi-class case, the applicant can divide the application so that the portion which has not been objected to can issue. Other possibilities are noted below.

The applicant may want to abandon the application and refile, hoping to get an examiner who is more receptive and gain

---

[14] Usually the applicant will hedge by saying "at least as early as. . . ."
[15] If a non-final action is issued, that does not mean that the applicant is making headway — it may be that the examiner is merely posturing for appeal. Certainly this is the case if the examiner cites a number of cases or conducts a common law database search.
[16] This is sometimes used as a tool to get additional evidence in the file for purposes of appeal.

another opportunity to reargue the issues. Alternatively, the applicant may decide to apply in a different format or to forego getting a registration and use the mark on a common law basis.

NOTICE OF APPEAL

If the applicant decides to appeal, the applicant must file a notice of appeal and pay an appeal fee. The applicant then must submit an Appeal Brief (this takes some effort and is where the applicant can cite and argue cases), and then the examiner decides whether to hold ground or cave. If the former, the examiner will file a reply brief. A decision is then made by the Trademark Trial and Appeal Board based on the two briefs. The applicant has the option of asking for an oral hearing. Appealing, for the most part, is a fruitless process, unless the examiner has totally screwed up, since it will merely result in the examiner being confirmed.[17]

THE INFAMOUS BLACKOUT PERIOD

"The Blackout Period" is the period during which proof of use will *not* be accepted for an ITU application. The blackout period begins the day after a mark is approved for publication. It ends upon issue of the notice of allowance. If an ITU application has been filed, at some point it will be necessary to either provide proof of use, or to amend the application to a use-based application. However, if the applicant files during the blackout period, the proofs that were filed will be rejected.

AMENDMENT TO THE SUPPLEMENTAL REGISTER

Amending to the Supplemental Register is easy. The applicant just sends in a letter amendment requesting that the words "Principal Register" be changed to "Supplemental Register."[18] An intent to use applicant has to allege use or submit a statement of use *before*

---

[17] The examiner is confirmed in about eighty percent of the cases.
[18] The applicant can also amend in the opposite direction. However, the applicant cannot switch a supplemental application to an intent to use application.

amending to the Supplemental Register. Amendments to the Supplemental Register cannot be made after appeal has been taken from a refusal to register on the Principal Register.

DISCLAIMERS

The examiner may require the applicant to disclaim unregistrable components from a mark. Also, the applicant may voluntarily disclaim portions of the mark.

The standard form of a disclaimer reads: "No claim is made to the exclusive right to use (insert the word or words) apart from the mark as shown." Other forms of waiver can be proposed. For example, frequently a statement is added to the effect that "common law rights to (the word or words) are not being waived." If two words are hyphenated or run together, the resulting mark is considered unitary, and disclaimer of its parts is unnecessary.

DIVISION OF APPLICATION

Just as multiple classes can be grouped into one application, so too can a case be divided again. One reason to do this is to issue classes which may be allowed, while appealing or abandoning the classes which were rejected.

NOTICE OF ALLOWANCE FOR USE-BASED APPLICATIONS

When the examiner has finished examining a use-based application, a notice of allowance will issue, and the application is passed to publication where it is published for opposition.

NOTICE OF PUBLICATION FOR INTENT TO USE APPLICATIONS

When the examiner has completed the first phase of examination, the application is sent to publication. This starts the black-out period.

PUBLICATION

An important part of the examination process is to give third parties a chance to oppose. The applicant will receive a notice from the Patent and Trademark Office stating when publication in the *Official Gazette* will take place and give the applicant an opportunity to acquire a copy. Notice of intent to file opposition must be filed within thirty days of publication. This is not much time to act, and usually a party considering opposing will take an extension of thirty or sixty days on top of this.[19]

NOTICE OF ALLOWANCE FOR INTENT TO USE APPLICATIONS

For intent to use applications, if no one opposes, a notice of allowance will issue. A notice of allowance requires that a statement of use be submitted within six months. The applicant can receive an automatic extension of six months (one year total from the publication date) by making a motion and paying a fee (currently $100 per class.)[20] Additional extensions up to one year (total two years from the publication date) are possible upon payment of additional fees and showing good cause.

STATEMENT OF USE

A statement of use is an amendment to allege use by another name, and the applicant provides the same verified statement, specimens and fee. (See Chapter Six for the forms of specimens.) In submitting the statement of use, any goods or services recited in the application in excess of those for which use is claimed should be canceled.

When the applicant submits proof of use, the goods should be limited to those actually being sold under the trademark.[21] If

---

[19] The maximum time allowed is 120 days from the publication date.

[20] The beauty of this system is that the applicant does not have to market a product until after the application has been examined and clears opposition.

[21] Proof of use only needs to be provided for one item in each class.

other goods are later developed, additional trademark filings can be made.[22]

REGISTRATION

If the application is use-based, a registration will normally issue several months after the opposition period has ended. For intent to use cases, it is first necessary that proofs of use be submitted. Only when the proofs of use are accepted, will a registration issue.

Registrations are valid for ten years and are renewable.[23] There is no issue fee as with patents. Upon registration, the application is considered to have been effective as of its filing date. Proof of use of the trademark is required during the sixth year. Fees are required in connection with the proof of use and the renewals.

LETTERS OF PROTEST

Protests from third parties who object to the issuance of a mark go to the Director of the Trademark Examining Groups who decides whether to inform the examiners. A letter of protest cannot be used as a means to delay ex parte prosecution or circumvent opposition or cancellation. Usually the protests are not acted on unless there is a clear error. This procedure is considered an indirect way to oppose and is normally a fruitless effort.

The Director acts on the protest, and the most the examiner sees, if anything, is a summary. The best time for a letter of protest to be filed is before publication. Protests filed more than thirty days after publication will generally be rejected.

---

[22] With copyrights there can only be one registration per subject matter and there can only be one patent per invention. However, with trademarks, you can obtain any number of registrations for a mark so long as the goods or form of the mark are different.

[23] Actually the registrant gets a longer initial term than ten years, since the registration relates back to the filing date.

ATTACK ON THIRD-PARTY REGISTRATIONS

During prosecution of the case, an applicant cannot attack the validity of a third party registration. The proper procedure to dispose of a reference is to file an action for cancellation which will result in the applicant's case being placed in abeyance pending its determination. Citation of a reference against an application gives the applicant standing to bring the cancellation.[24]

CONSENT AGREEMENTS

In the context of prosecution, consent agreements are submitted in situations where a mark has been rejected on a registration and the applicant goes to the owner and obtains a consent to register. The applicant sends a copy to the examiner and requests that the rejection be withdrawn. In a shift of policy, the Trademark Office has indicated that the examiners should give the consents due consideration.

CROSS REFERENCES

For formal requirements for filing applications, see Chapter Six. ITU applications are discussed in Chapter Five.

---

[24] In bringing a cancellation, the applicant should ask the examiner to put his application in abeyance (suspend prosecution) until a decision is reached on the cancellation.

Eight

Post-Issue Procedures

Federal trademark registrations do not have constitutionally limited terms like copyrights and patents, and can last so long as they are properly maintained. Once a registration lapses, however, it cannot be revived, but must be cloned by filing and issuing a new registration.[1]

The terms for Federal registrations run in continuous segments, depending in which act they were issued under. Registrations which were obtained, or had been renewed, under the Lanham Act *before November 16, 1989* have terms of twenty years. *Registrations that have issued or have been renewed since then have terms of ten years.*[2]

> **TERMS OF PRIOR ACTS**
>
> The Trademark Act of 1905 had twenty-year terms. The Trademark Act of 1881 had thirty-year original terms and renewed for twenty-year terms. The Act of 1920 had no term and registrations were not subject to renewal. The Lanham Act (1946) had twenty-year terms and twenty-year renewals, which were reduced to ten years by the 1989 Act.

Proof of use and payment of fees are required during the sixth year of the original term by filing a declaration of use under Section 8, and at the end of the term, if the registration is to be renewed, by filing an application for renewal under Section

---

[1] The new registration will have a new filing date and the priority date of the earlier case will have been lost.

[2] §8. Registrations which were in their initial term on November 16, 1989 remain in force for twenty years, assuming a Section 8 Declaration is filed during the sixth year.

9.[3] A Section 8 declaration is required *during* the sixth year to show use of the trademark, and if this is not submitted, the registration will lapse.[4] Section 9 declarations are required at the end of the original terms and at the end of each renewal term. *A Section 9 declaration must be filed within a nine-month window starting six months before a registration lapses and ending three months after the term has expired.*[5]

Lapse of a registration without further information does not indicate abandonment of the trademark. Someone could merely have improperly docketed the renewal, or decided it was an unnecessary expense. The registration was not necessary to support the applicant's common law rights, and the common law rights may continue unabated.

The registrant can also file a Section 15 declaration. Section 15 declarations are usually filed at the same time as Section 8 declarations. A Section 15 declaration is permissive and gives a registration "incontestability." Since most applicants want to achieve this status early-on, conventional practice is to file a combined Section 8 and 15 declaration of use and incontestability soon after the start of the sixth year. Not filing a Section 8 or Section 9 declaration will void the registration, but has no affect on the underlying trademark.

The following scenario illustrates typical post-issue procedures. George obtains a trademark registration for "BLUE BOY" for men's shorts in Int. Class 25. The registration certificate shows the date of application, the date of issue and the number of the certificate. The registration has a term of *ten years* and issued on January 15, 1993. Printed on the certificate is a notice of the Section 8 requirements. Time slips by. George is still selling "BLUE BOY" shorts. He checks into renewal proceedings which he un-

---

[3] The author prefers declarations, since they can be executed anywhere any time without being concerned over local formalities.

[4] The six-year term is measured from the registration date and not the filing date. Since a trademark is a reference as of the application date, the trademark owner really has a longer initial term than six years since the period it is pending registration is tacked on for free. Perhaps at some point the law will be changed so that the term of a trademark runs from the application date, as has been done for patents.

[5] §9

derstands is due after ten years. What did George forget? The Section 8 declaration. When was that due? The Section 8 declaration was required during the sixth year of the term, i.e., between January 15, 1998 and January 15, 1999. Since this deadline was missed, the registration lapsed.

What if a party obtains a registration and then fails to market products under the mark? Non-use of a registered trademark for a period of *three years* leads to a statutory presumption of abandonment of its registration.[6] However, the registration will not flush itself, and a cancellation action must be filed to remove it from the register.

If a registrant files the Section 8 declaration and it is accepted, the registrant must maintain the registration again during the tenth year by submitting proof of use and a declaration under Section 9. Thereafter, the trademark registrations must be maintained (renewed) at intervals of ten years by paying a fee and showing proof of use in commerce.[7]

SECTION 8 DECLARATIONS

Registrations on both the Principal and Supplemental Registers require Section 8 declarations.[8] Section 8 declarations must be filed during the sixth year of the term of the trademark:

The registration of any mark under the provisions of this Act shall be canceled by the Commissioner at the end of six years following its date, unless within one year next preceding the expiration of such six years the registrant shall file in the Patent and Trademark Office an affidavit showing that the mark is in use in commerce or showing that its nonuse is due to special circumstances which excuse the nonuse and is not due to any attention to abandon the mark.[9]

---

[6] This was changed, effective January 1, 1996, from two years under GATT.

[7] Most foreign countries do not require proof of use for renewal.

[8] The difference between declarations and affidavits is that the former is based on a statutory oath while the latter is done before a notary. Declarations are usually done because they are simpler. However, their legal affect is the same.

[9] §8(a)

If the registrant files prematurely, the declaration is no good. If it is filed too late, it will be rejected. Also, registrants should avoid the trap of executing the declaration early, and filing on time since this is still grounds for rejection. Therefore, the declaration is only valid if both made and filed after the expiration of five years and before the end of the sixth year.

The declaration or affidavit must: (1) state that the mark is in use in commerce; (2) list the goods or services with which the mark is in use in commerce and (3) specify the nature of the commerce.[10] A statutory fee is required for each class and proofs of current use are needed for each class.[11]

While the statute has a provision for explaining nonuse, registrants should not rely on this, since as it is unlikely to work, and it provides a basis for future attack. In this situation, it is best for the registrant to use the trademark and maintain it, or let the original application lapse and reapply during its pendency so that the registrant will maintain priority rights on record.

Declarations should be made by the owner of record. If the owner of record is no longer the owner because of an assignment of the mark, the title should be corrected. *Also, the goods or services must be limited to those actually still in use with the mark.*

RENEWALS

Renewals, or Section 9 declarations, are filed at the end of the original term of grant, i.e., at the end of ten or twenty years. Renewal applications must be filed within the six month period before the lapse of the registration, or within three months thereafter. Filing within the three-month period after the lapse of the registration requires payment of a penalty.[12]

The declaration or affidavit must set forth the goods or services in each class with which the mark is still in use in commerce, specifying the nature of the commerce.[13] A specimen is required for each class showing current use, and a fee for each

---

[10] Rule 2.162

[11] The fee is $100 per class. Proofs of use need only be prepared for one item per class.

[12] The penalty for filing late is $100 per class.

[13] Rule 2.183

class is required. If there are goods listed in the registration for which the mark is no longer used, these must be deleted.

The renewal term is for ten years, and there is no cap on the number of possible renewals.[14] So long as the registrant keeps making renewals, the registration will last indefinitely (assuming the law doesn't change.)

SPECIMENS

Specimens are required for Section 8 and 9 declarations. Proofs of use of the trademark must be attached to the forms.[15] If the trademark is in block letter form, proof of use in any style will generally support it. If the trademark is in stylized form, proof of use in the same form is required. The specimen should reflect proof of use of the mark in commerce. The registrant must specify the particular kind of commerce in the Declaration, i.e., describe whether the commerce is interstate or foreign. Only one specimen is required per class.

LEGITIMATE USE

The use in commerce required to support Section 8 and 9 declarations and renewals must be legitimate use in ordinary trade. Token use to maintain a registration no longer suffices.

What if the current specimens differ from the drawing of the mark? Whether it will be accepted or not depends on the degree of difference. A material alteration will result in the proof being refused. Changes in background, styling or modernization do not generally result in rejection.[16]

---

[14] The renewal fee is $300 per class. Other countries have renewals too, except they generally charge higher fees.

[15] Previously, three proofs were required; now only one is necessary.

[16] The registrant may want to fax a copy of the altered mark to the Trademark Office to solicit their comments in advance of making a formal submission.

SECTION 15 DECLARATIONS

Section 15 declarations relate to incontestability rather than term extension. Section 15 declarations: (1) confirm the right of the registrant to use the mark in commerce for goods and services for which it was registered and (2) make a mark incontestable, i.e., no other party can attack it based on descriptiveness or prior use. In making a Section 15 declaration, the registrant makes a statement: (1) that the goods or services have been in continuous use for the immediately preceding five years and (2) that there has been no final decision adverse to the registrant's claim of ownership or right to register or any pending proceeding involving said right. The registrant is required as part of the declaration to identify those goods in the registration on which the mark has been in continuous use in commerce.

Achieving incontestability is important. Incontestability is a major event in the life of the trademark registration — like coming of age. It is an indication that the mark is mature and survived its childhood years. Up until this point, any prior user could challenge the registration. The filing fee for a Section 15 declaration is $100 per class. The fee for combined Section 8 and 15 declarations is $200 per class.

Consider the following scenario. Mike opened a chain of bagel shops named "MAD MIKE'S" on the West Coast and obtained a federal service mark for restaurant services in Int. Class 42. This gives Mike priority rights throughout the U.S. However, some low profile user in a remote part of the country could defeat the registration. If five years pass without anyone contesting the service mark, and a Section 15 Declaration is filed and accepted, pre-existing users are no longer a threat.

SURRENDER, CANCELLATION OR AMENDMENT

With regard to surrender, cancellation and amendment of registered marks, the law states that:

Upon application by the registrant, the Commissioner may permit any registration to be surrendered for cancellation.... Upon application of the registrant and payment of the prescribed fees, the Commissioner for good cause may permit a registration to be amended or disclaimed in part; provided, however, that the amendment or disclaimer does not materially alter the character of the mark. [17]

There is no fee for voluntary surrender of a registration. Also, classes can be canceled. The original certificate of registration should be returned. If the original certificate is lost, a written explanation should be provided.

No substantial amendment to the mark is permitted, but a small change may be accepted and then the registrant has a new reference point and another small change is possible.[18] No amendment to the goods or services can be made, except to restrict (delete) items.

RE-REGISTRATION OF MARKS UNDER PRIOR ACTS

Trademarks obtained under the Acts of 1905 and 1881 can be reexamined and republished and converted into Lanham Act applications under Section 12(c). Some registrants convert their applications in order to make them incontestable.

The converted applications are republished in the *Official Gazette* and are re-registered. After five years of continuous use, a Section 15 declaration can be filed.[19]

CORRECTION OF PTO MISTAKES

There is no monopoly on mistakes, and the Patent and Trademark Office contributes its share. If a registrant catches them making one, they will correct it without charge. This is why registrants should always proofread the certificate of registration.[20]

---

[17] §7(e)

[18] The registrant may compare the original drawing to the form of the mark now being used, and the differences may appear significant. However, if incremental changes were made over a period of years, any individual change may have been proper.

[19] Docketing will be confusing because the registrant will still have the basic term ticking from the original issue date, not the date of the registration.

[20] §7(g). Particularly, the registrant should check the mark, the registrant's name and the statement of goods and services.

CORRECTION OF APPLICANT'S MISTAKE

If a mistake was made in good faith, correction is permitted, unless republication is required. [21]

CERTIFICATE ISSUED TO THE ASSIGNEE

If a trademark registration is assigned to one party, and title is in another party, the assignee can have a new certificate of registration prepared and issued to another party for the unexpired part of the original term. [22]

REISSUE OF CERTIFICATE TO ASSIGNEE

If the registration is issued when it assigned, it can still be reissued in the assignee's name.[23] The original certificate should be turned in. Most companies merely correct the chain of title and do not go this far.

CROSS REFERENCES

See Appendices Twelve and Thirteen for Section 8 and 15 and Section 9 declaration forms.

---

[21] §7(h)
[22] §7(d)
[23] Rule 2.171.

Nine

Policing Trademarks

Trademarks must be policed so that the rights acquired at common law, or by registration, are not lost. Policing is the responsibility of the trademark owner; it is part of owning trademarks. Some companies or organizations have representatives whose sole job is to police the market for infringing trademarks. Now, with unregistered trademarks and trade dress federally protected, owners need to police in these areas as well.

WHAT TO DO WITH A REGISTRATION CERTIFICATE

What do you do with the certificate of registration? Do you put it in a safe or frame it to hang on your study wall? There is no problem with either of these actions, but what steps do you need to take to safeguard the registration? The following is a list of steps to consider taking:
• notify others in the company about what trademark notation to use in advertising and on the product labels.
• check to see if there are any infringers and give warning notices to them.
• record the registration with Customs.
• docket for a Section 8 declaration.
• notify licensees.

Federal trademark registrations are not always respected. The trademark owner needs to constantly monitor the marketplace for third parties who are using the mark improperly. Counterfeit products undoubtedly take away part of the trademark owner's market share and destroy the mark's goodwill. There is also the possibility that third parties are selling products that, although not counterfeit, may be confusingly similar. And if the mark is distinctive, the trademark owner has to be concerned about the use of the mark on collateral products as well.

Furthermore, the new trademark owner may encounter parties who are using the registered trademark as a generic name or descriptively, or who are not using proper legal notices. Trademarks can be lost if the trademark owner allows the public to use them anyway they want. No set of instructions or maintenance material comes with a registration, and frequently trademark owners do not learn about their mistakes until they go to court. Trademark owners have two choices: either police their trademark or lose their rights.

RULES OF POLICING

Trademark policing starts and ends with the owner. The owner has got to know the basic rules of policing and must spread the word among employees, licensees and franchisees. In addition, the trademark owner needs to make sure that the mark is not being misrepresented through the media.

Licensees and franchisees act as the trademark owner's extensions, and if they misrepresent the mark in any way, it will diminish the owner's goodwill and the value of the mark. Their products and services must meet the owner's standards and specifications. For this reason, quality control is the number one concern of the trademark owner.

The trademark owner must also watch for applicants and infringers of confusingly similar marks. It is mandatory for the trademark owner to watch the marks being registered or applied for, in order to file oppositions and cancellations, or to bring infringement actions.[1]

The trademark owner must make sure that the mark is used correctly in the media. The owner needs to be vigilant in making sure that the mark is not used descriptively or generically, or for goods or services for which it is not registered.

TRADEMARK AUDIT CHECKLIST

The following checklist was developed to enable trademark owners to audit use of their trademarks both within the company and by outside parties.

---

[1] Infringements result when the products are being or have been sold under a confusingly similar mark.

- **Find out what names or symbols are claimed as trademarks and service marks and for what products and services.** Before investigating third parties, trademark owners need to know what marks their companies or units are supposed to have. The trademark owner needs to see if the products and services being provided match the claimed goods and services. Often there will be a gap in coverage or the mark is found to be used in a different form than shown in the registration. The trademark owner needs to decide if the registrations should be amended, or if new trademark applications need to be filed.

- **Make sure a trademark is used as a trademark and a service mark is used as a service mark in connection with the claimed goods and services.** It is not enough to have a mark and corresponding goods or services. No rights attach unless correct trademark usage is made. This means using the mark in a trademark sense on the product, its packaging or displays, or in the case of a service mark, in advertising.

- **Make sure the mark is used in a distinctive form and as an adjective rather than a noun.** Grammatically speaking, a trademark is a proper adjective. The mark should be written distinctively and usually will have an initial capitalized letter or all capitalized letters. The name of the goods it is used with should follow the mark.[2] While it is not necessary to use the same product name in every situation, it is desirable to have an approved short list of acceptable nouns to work from.

- **Make sure that all trademarks are properly designated. All federally registered marks should always include the "circle R" designation.**[3] While use of a trademark designator is not required, significant legal advantages result from its use — namely, the trademark owner can recover damages and lost profits from infringers.[4]

---

[2] The name of the goods does not have to appear on the actual product because the tangible product equates to the noun, i.e., the purchaser can see for him- or herself what the goods are.

[3] §29. Usually this will be as a superscript. Alternative notice forms are available, e.g., "Registered in the U.S. Patent and Trademark Office," or "Reg. U.S. Pat. & Tm. Off."

[4] However, there is a risk of misuse being found if the "Circle R" is affixed before the mark is federally registered for the goods and services in question.

> ## SM AND TM
>
> **"SM"** customarily stands for service mark and **"TM"** for trademark. They are used often, but they don't offer any legal advantage. There are no statutory restrictions on their use. They may be used with common law marks, applications and registrations. Their main benefit is to warn others that the owner is claiming trademark rights to the identified mark.

• **Exercise quality control over products produced by, or services performed by, licensees and affiliates.** Subsidiaries are considered to be wholly-owned, and affiliates are owned less than 100 percent, but not less than 50 percent. Control by a parent over subsidiaries is assumed.[5] But for licensees and affiliates, evidence of a written license agreement with appropriate quality control and trademark usage provisions is required.[6]

• **Monitor the market for third parties who may be using confusingly similar marks for the same or related goods or services.** There can only be one source behind a trademark, which means that the trademark owner has to keep the field clean. If the owner allows other parties to co-exist using a similar mark, the trademark is doomed for destruction.

• **Write cease and desist letters and bring infringement actions as necessary to prevent the likelihood of public confusion.**[7] When the trademark owner has written cease and desist letters and followed up aggressively, legal action should be considered, since some parties will not respond until the issue is forced. One factor of significance is the location of the infringer, since remote users cannot be sued until there is an overlap in the market territories.

---

[5] §5

[6] What counts is actual control. If the trademark owner has this, the written agreement is not needed. The optimum procedure is to have both a written agreement and actual control.

[7] The author's practice is to send certified (return receipt) letters and to follow up with telegrams or faxes. A litigator can be brought in at the next level, but be sure to weigh the risks. If the party is accessible, a personal visit may be in order. Sometimes it is desirable to have a private investigator do this. Basically, there are no set rules.

• **Monitor the federal registry to see what marks are being registered or applied for by the competition.** The *Official Trademark Gazette* is published weekly. By watching to see what intent to use cases are being filed, trademark owners can get valuable information about their competitors.

• **Bring oppositions and cancellations as required to keep the federal registries clear of potentially infringing marks.** Keeping the federal registries clear is important. The trademark owner might tolerate some local users, but if someone gets a federal registration, this could erode or restrict the owner's rights and could be used as a reference against subsequent filings.

• **File intent to use applications.** The best way to protect trademarks is an aggressive filing program. This puts everyone on notice that the applicant is claiming a potential trademark for the stated goods and services and gives the applicant territorial rights throughout the U.S. Intent to use applications allow the applicant to protect a potential trademark for all areas of the U.S. before any marketing program is instituted.

TRADEMARK LICENSES

If the trademark is licensed, it is the responsibility of the trademark owner to see that the products manufactured or services offered by the licensee meet specified quality control standards. If the owner does not control the quality, the public will receive inferior products, and the goodwill to the mark will suffer. Whether the owner grants exclusive or non-exclusive rights makes no difference — quality must be strictly and carefully controlled. Third parties, affiliates and joint venture partners using the mark should be covered. Since use by wholly-owned subsidiaries inures to the parent, licenses are not technically required, but it is still good practice.[8] (See Chapter Twelve.)

MONITORING THE *OFFICIAL GAZETTE*

Since filing is equivalent to use and gives other parties priority rights as of their filing dates, trademark owners need to

---

[8] For example, what if the subsidiary operates outside the U.S.? Without a formal license, the situation would be unclear.

periodically monitor the Federal Trademark Register to determine whether anyone has filed on one of their trademarks and to keep tabs on competition.

OPPOSITIONS AND CANCELLATIONS

Keeping the registers clear of conflicting marks is important. This is achieved by monitoring federal applications and filing any necessary oppositions and cancellations. Oppositions are filed against trademark applications following publication in the *Official Gazette*. Cancellations are actions against registered trademarks.

With the availability of intent to use filings, applicants who file may have not fully introduced their product and have just begun test marketing. This is good news for the trademark owner, since it is generally easier to get potential infringers to cease when they are trying to register than to try to stop them after they have begun selling products. Therefore, the trademark owner will want to be aggressive in bringing inter parte actions.

THIRD PARTY TRADEMARK USE

Disputes follow successful trademarks as surely as night follows day. Infringers can pop up anytime.[9] When this happens, investigation of the infringing company should begin right away. The trademark owner should investigate how long the infringing trademark has been marketed or the business has been in operation.[10] A prior user will be able to continue use within his territory irrespective of any trademark registration. Also, there is a risk that the party may attack a subsequent registration.

If the trademark owner is confident of priority, he or she should send a certified, return receipt letter to the party, requesting that the party cease using the trademark. Usually, the trademark owner should agree to allow a reasonable period of time for the party to phase out use of the trademark.

---

[9] Database screening is a good way to find new companies that may be using a registered trademark.

[10] There is always the danger that the so-called infringer has been using the trademark all along. The trademark owner should avoid making threats where someone may have an earlier date of use.

The important thing is to exercise due diligence to protect the goodwill associated with the trademark by eliminating the infringing mark. If that is accomplished, the trademark owner can afford to be flexible as to when this is accomplished. If the party does not concede, the trademark owner should escalate matters by having an attorney send a cease and desist letter. If this does not produce results, an infringement suit should be considered.[11] If the party has filed a federal trademark application, this may provide a suitable forum for attacking the party.

MEDIA USAGE OF MARKS

Monitoring magazines and newspapers isn't glamorous, but it is essential in properly policing the market for infringers. As stated earlier, trademarks are proper adjectives and should modify a noun which generically represents the goods or services. If any form of media coverage refers to a trademark as a noun or in a generic way, the trademark owner needs to take action. Similarly, the trademark owner needs to make sure that the proper trademark notation is used, and that the mark is used with the correct goods and services.

Also, as the owner is looking through magazines and newspapers, it is not a bad idea to check competitor's advertising. If a competitor is misstating facts about products or services, the trademark owner may have a cause of action.

MARKS USED AS TRADE NAMES

Another important aspect to policing is to make sure all uses of the mark are made with the owner's permission and preferably under a written agreement. Trading name agreements must exist for subsidiaries, affiliates and joint venture partners using the trademark in their name.

---

[11] It is desirable to check the company again just before suit is filed, to verify that the infringement is continuing. On several occasions, the author has found that the infringer had stopped using the trademark while the complaint was being drafted.

COLLATERAL PRODUCTS

If a trademark owner allows a manufacturer to put its logo or other trademark on T-shirts and other collateral products, the transaction is a license, which means a vendor's agreement is required. This can be a short form agreement, but should clearly have quality control provisions.[12]

DESIGN MANUAL AND TRADEMARK GUIDE

Every company, large or small, should have a design manual or style guide to use as a reference standard when design issues arise. A design manual establishes the company image and identity. In addition to a corporate design manual, a company will often have design or usage manuals for the company's trademarks. These identify the company's trademarks and explain rules of usage, e.g., a trademark should be accompanied by a product descriptor and be used with an initial capitalized letter. This manual will also describe when and how the "Circle R" designation will be used.

CROSS REFERENCES

See Chapter Ten on inter partes actions, Chapter Twelve on licensing and Chapter Seventeen on infringement actions.

---

[12] The agreement can be used, for example, to support the manufacture of a company logo for clothing items. Chapter Twelve includes a sample vendor's agreement in its Addendum.

Ten

Inter Partes Actions

Inter partes actions are oppositions, cancellations, concurrent use proceedings and interferences. An inter partes proceeding is where two opposing parties battle for rights and the Trademark Trial and Appeals Board acts as an impartial judge and referee.

Oppositions allow a party who has standing to attack a pending trademark application. Cancellations are used to invalidate an issued registration. In a concurrent use proceeding, registrations are granted to different parties for different territories. Interferences, while still in the law, are now only of historical note.

The timing of an opposition is critical. Notice of opposition has to be filed within a designated time of publication of the trademark in the *Official Gazette*. Cancellations can be filed at any time once the mark has been registered and any time thereafter. Concurrent use proceedings must be instituted while at least one party has a *pending* application covering the trademark.

Inter partes proceedings are conducted according to the Rules of Federal Civil Procedure, except that some special rules prescribed by the Trademark Office are applicable. The parties conduct discovery, which can include written and oral interrogatories, requests for admissions and requests for documents. Testimony is taken by oral or written interrogatories.[1] Briefs are filed, and an oral hearing can be requested.

Decisions are made by a three-judge panel of the Trademark Trial and Appeals Board. After the decision is rendered, a request for rehearing can be filed. The losing party can appeal or seek a trial de novo.

Inter partes proceedings are legally technical, costly and time-consuming. This chapter was included so that readers will

---

[1] Depositions are taken in the district where the deponent resides or is regularly employed.

have background information on this subject; not so that readers can attempt to handle these matters themselves. You've undoubtedly heard the saying that the attorney who represents him- or herself has a fool for a client. Applicants or registrants who try to represent themselves in oppositions and cancellations are equally foolish. However, anyone who wants to try will need to purchase a copy of the *Trademark Trial and Appeal Board Manual of Procedure*, which is available from the government printing office. The author's advice: engage an experienced trademark attorney and be a "Texican," i.e., an early settler.

OPPOSITIONS

When a mark has been applied for on the Principal Register and has been approved by the Examiner, it is published weekly in the *Trademark Official Gazette*. This gives the public an opportunity to object. If anyone considers the mark to be descriptive or generic, or confusingly similar to a mark he or she owns, a Notice of Opposition can be filed.

This allows the parties who believe that they will be harmed by a registration to attack the applicant's right to obtain the registration. Oppositions filed by different parties are prosecuted individually, and each opposer must establish his own rights.

NOTICE OF OPPOSITION

When opposing an application, the Federal Rules §8(a) requires that the opposer or pleader make "a short plain statement of the claim showing that the pleader is entitled to relief." To comply, the opposer needs only to set forth a short and plain statement showing how he or she would be damaged by the registration of the opposed mark and state the grounds of opposition. An original and duplicate of the notice of opposition must be filed in the U.S. Patent and Trademark Office together with the required filing fee (currently $200.) The opposer should keep pleadings to a minimum, since during discovery the opposer will be asked to provide documentation to support his or her allegations. The Notice of Opposition can be filed by the opposer's attorney.

Initially, a party has thirty days to oppose; however, this period can be extended up to 120 days. The opposer begins the opposition by filing a written Notice of Opposition with the Trademark Office. An opposer has to demonstrate a personal interest in the outcome beyond that of the general public, i.e., the opposer must establish *standing* by showing a commercial link.[2]

Attacks on an application can be made based on:

(1) likelihood of confusion;
(2) descriptiveness or genericness;
(3) misdecriptiveness or deceptiveness; or
(4) fraud.

Claims of dilution, unfair competition or false advertising are not considered by the Board. Prior use can be based on use as a trademark, trade name or in advertising. Interstate use is not required to oppose. The applicant's goods or services listed in the application are controlling.[3] It is irrelevant what goods the applicant may be manufacturing, is intending to manufacture or has covered in other applications.

CANCELLATIONS

Cancellations are actions which are brought in the U.S. Patent and Trademark Office against *registered* marks on the Principal and Supplemental Registers. These proceedings are similar to oppositions, except that instead of filing a Notice of Opposition, the petitioner files a Petition for Cancellation. Until a trademark has become incontestable under a Section 15 declaration, it is subject to attack for any of the reasons that an application could have been attacked during the opposition period. *Once a Section 15 declaration is accepted, the grounds of attack based on descriptiveness, misdecriptiveness and likelihood of confusion with previously used marks or prior registrations are statutorily precluded.*

---

[2] One good way to show direct harm is if the application was rejected by the Trademark Office because of the opposing party's application or registration.

[3] Even for intent to use filings, one still looks at the listed goods and services. It makes no difference that the applicant has had no actual use.

However, cancellations can still be brought against incontestable marks for the following reasons:

(1) the mark is generic;

(2) the mark has been abandoned;

(3) the registration was obtained by fraud;

(4) the mark comprises immoral, scandalous or deceptive matter;

(5) the mark comprises national insignia;

(6) the mark comprises the names of living individuals or U.S. presidents;

(7) the mark is an improperly-used collective or certification mark;

(8) the mark disparages or falsely suggests a connection with persons, institutions, beliefs or national symbols; or

(9) The mark is used to misrepresent the source of goods.[4]

Therefore, regardless of how long a registration has been in force, and its incontestability notwithstanding, it can be attacked. Genericness, abandonment and suggestion of false connection represent the greatest hazards. For this reason, the trademark owner never reaches a point of safety where his or her guard can be let down. Trademarks require continuous use, maintenance and protection; they can never be put aside in a closet and forgotten.

SUPPLEMENTAL REGISTRATIONS

Supplemental registrations cannot be opposed, but they can be canceled for reasons other than descriptiveness. Should they be attacked? If they are confusingly similar to an opposer's mark, the opposer should at least write a letter of protest.

Generally, the party who acquires a Supplemental Registration will keep on coming. He'll likely try to register the mark on the Principal Register at some point. That is good reason for the opposer to establish a claim. Prudence dictates that the opposer should go after the Supplemental Registration as soon as possible.

---

[4] This has to be more than likelihood of confusion.

THE ANSWER

The answers to either an opposition or cancellation are similar and are due within forty days of mailing.[5] If the action is an opposition, the party answering is called the "Respondent." If the action is a cancellation, the party answering is the "Registrant."

The answer must admit, deny or plead lack of knowledge of each allegation in the Notice of Opposition or Petition for Cancellation. Any equitable defenses of laches, estoppel or acquiescence must be pleaded. A counterclaim to cancel the opposer or petitioner's registration is mandatory.

CONCURRENT USE PROCEEDINGS

A concurrent use proceeding results in a trademark registration being divided so that two or more parties are accorded different territorial rights. Applications by both parties or an application and a registration are required. Concurrent use proceedings do not occur with the frequency of oppositions or cancellations, but they do occur often enough that the trademark owner should be aware of them. Threaten someone for infringement in a remote territory and a concurrent use proceeding could result. A concurrent use proceeding can also result from an opposition, but not from a cancellation.

INTERFERENCES

There will probably never be another trademark interference.[6] This procedure is a carryover from patent law to determine priority of use between two applicants for the same mark or between an applicant and a registrant. Supplemental Register registrations and Principal Register registrations that have become incontestable are not subject to interference. Priority rests with the first party to use or file. The junior party has the bur-

---

[5] See the date stamped on the letter from the Patent and Trademark Office.

[6] The last decision reporting a trademark interference was in 1974. *In re Family of Am., Inc.*, 180 USPQ 332 (Comm'r Pat. 1974).

den of proof. An interference can only be declared by the Commissioner upon a petitioner showing extraordinary circumstances. The position of the Patent and Trademark Office is that inter partes matters are best determined by oppositions and cancellations.

APPEAL PROCESSES

There are several options involving appeal processes in inter partes proceedings. The first step begins with the Trademark Trial and Appeal Board. Where the parties go from there depends on their financial resources, how good a case they have and their strategy.

If a party loses before the Board, that party can request a rehearing. If a party loses the rehearing, appeal can be made either to the Court of Appeals for the Federal Circuit (CAFC) or to the district court for a trial de novo. In the CAFC, appeal is on the record. In the district court, new evidence can be introduced, and the parties can seek injunctions. Survey evidence is often crucial and going the district court route can allow a party to design a new survey and introduce it. Another consideration is that the appellant will most likely end up on the defendant's home court.

SETTLEMENT

Usually, the parties are better off if a settlement can be reached, and this is encouraged by the Board. Sometimes the applicant or registrant is content to use the mark without obtaining a registration. The parties then draw up a settlement agreement putting limits on the use or on the goods and services so that the public will not be confused.

If a party has filed abroad, a global settlement agreement should be considered.[7] Rarely will one party win everywhere, and a settlement at some point will have to be reached before either party can market effectively.

---

[7] While many foreign countries have oppositions, because of the discovery process, the U.S. is the most difficult, except perhaps for Canada. Usually the parties only submit written arguments to the local trademark office, and a decision is rendered.

CROSS REFERENCES

See litigation, Chapter Seventeen. The Addendum lists inter partes survival rules.

ADDENDUM ONE: INTER PARTES SURVIVAL RULES

1. Have an experienced trademark attorney do your inter partes work. Someone handling a case pro se has no chance.

2. File intent to use applications early on to establish priority dates. If you are the applicant, it is preferable for oppositions to be filed against ITU applications, since you do not have to disclose any sales information, or risk there being instances of actual confusion in the marketplace.

3. Search again before using a mark or filing; you may be surprised at what you find. You can never search too many times.

4. Monitor the *Official Gazette* or trademark databases for infringers. You are charged with statutory notice of filings. Therefore, you had better know what is out there.

5. Keep conflicting marks off the registers. It usually is more important to eliminate an application than to discontinue actual use.

6. Settle early and globally, if possible. A fair settlement is often better than a hard fought victory.

7. Keep in mind that whatever records you keep are likely discoverable.

8. Mark all communications with your attorney "Confidential . . . Client-Attorney Privilege."

9. The first user will prevail. The quickest way to be the first user is to file an ITU federal application. *This gives you constructive use as of the date of filing.*

10. Be alert for third party users. Someone may have priority over both parties. While irrelevant to the proceeding at hand, these rights can be acquired by the other party, or you may be able to hopscotch over the other party.

11. Read the *Official Gazette* religiously or have a law firm watch for conflicting marks.

12. Take an extension of time to oppose anytime you have concern about a mark. You may be able to resolve matters without filing a notice of opposition.

Eleven

Assignments

An assignment is a transfer of property rights which passes title to the purchaser or assignee. Statutory rules govern assignments of registrations. There can only be one party owning a mark, and a mark cannot be assigned without goodwill. Failure to comply with these conditions can result in abandonment. An "intent to use" application cannot be assigned during the time period in which the mark is sent to publication; the mark can only be assigned after a statement of use is filed. The mechanics for making an assignment and procedures for recordal are discussed below.

A trademark assignment is a transfer of title. The purchaser, or assignee, of a trademark stands in the place of the original owner. This means that the assignee will be entitled to claim the assignor's goodwill and priority dates.[1] Otherwise, the assignee would be starting anew and have to establish his or her own dates of use and goodwill. The Trademark Rules define an assignment as: ". . . the transfer of its (a party's) entire right, title, and interest in a registered mark or a mark for which an application to register has been filed.[2] Under the copyright laws, both assignments and exclusive licenses are defined as "transfers of ownership" and there is provision for multiple ownership. However, the divisibility of ownership does not apply to trademarks. *With trademarks, there is one owner and anyone else who has any interest in the mark is a licensee.*

---

[1] Otherwise, the assignee would be starting over from scratch, developing his own goodwill while hoping that there was no intervening party.

[2] Rules, §3.1. The same definition covers the assignment of a patent or patent application, except that it allows for an assignment of a partial interest as the entire interest. However, since trademarks are unitary, no partial assignment can be made.

The owner, whether identified or not, is the party that maintains overall control and quality of the products and services. The owner can be an individual, a corporation, a partnership, association or joint venture, a trust, etc., so long as it is a legally recognized entity. However, joint ownership of a mark is generally not permitted.

TRADEMARKS DON'T DIVIDE

Let's say that a partnership, which owns a solitary trademark registration, decides to dissolve. The parties have a falling out and want to divide the assets. Can they each own fifty percent of the registration? Not as individuals, as the mark would then have two sources. They could form a joint venture or corporation to hold title. Then, each would have fifty percent ownership interests through the joint venture or by stock ownership. Of course, if the parties do not get along, this isn't likely to work. In any case, if the parties don't deal with the situation, the mark will be abandoned and will become available to anyone.

Even exclusive licensees do not have ownership in a trademark. While an exclusive licensee can exercise quality control relative to sublicensees, there is a pyramid arrangement, and the exclusive licensee must be controlled by the owner.

Another characteristic feature of U.S. trademarks is that they *cannot be assigned or transferred without goodwill.*[3] If a business is involved, the mark can be sold with the business. However, what if the assignor is a distributor, or owns a portfolio of trademarks and has no separate assets to convey? Can the goodwill still be assigned? The assignment of a mark and goodwill has been upheld upon written contract, i.e., where there was no transfer of physical assets, or where the assignee was already in the same line of business. Therefore, the transfer of goodwill is dependent, not only on what the assignor has to assign, but also on

---

[3] While this is the rule in the U.S., goodwill usually is not considered abroad. There, trademarks are transferred in gross like other property rights.

the existing business of the assignee. If the assignee is in a different business, or uses the mark for different goods, the transfer becomes more tentative.

The ultimate test of whether the goodwill is in fact transferred is to compare the products and services prior to the transfer with those produced or provided by the assignee. If they are the same or similar, the public will not be deceived, and the transfer of goodwill is complete. If lesser quality goods are being sold or a different product is offered, the trademark will be jeopardized.

Where possible, supplemental materials supporting the transfer of goodwill should be acquired by the assignee, e.g., labels, product literature and specifications, customer lists, etc. It is the assignee who is at risk of having the trademark voided if sufficient goodwill is not transferred, and the duty is incumbent upon the assignee to obtain everything he or she needs to continue to produce products or provide services of the same quality offered by the assignor.

Another restriction concerning the transfer of trademarks is the prohibition against assigning "intent to use" applications until proof of use has been provided. The Lanham Act, Section 10, provides that:

> . . . no application to register a mark under Section 1(b) [intent to use], shall be assignable prior to the filing of the verified statement of use under Section 1(d), except to a successor of the business of the applicant, or portion thereof, to which the mark pertains, if that business is ongoing and existing.

Ordinarily, this would not pose a problem, since the applicant would be able to convert its Section 1(b) application to a Section 1(a) application. However, because of the *blackout period*, there is a substantial period of time when proof of use cannot be provided.[4] The trademark applicant must wait from when the application has been sent by the examiner to publication to

---

[4] Apparently, this provision resulted in order to prevent assignments where there had been no use and hence no goodwill had been developed.

when the examiner reacquires control of the case. This prohibition has an exception where the assignor's entire ongoing business is sold, or the entire portion of the business which involves the mark is sold.[5]

ASSIGNMENT PROVISIONS

Common law rights to a trademark can be assigned orally or in writing. Conversely, federal registrations can be sold only if assigned *in writing*, and the assignment of title must be recorded with the Trademark Office.[6] A typical assignment provision is as follows:

> Assignor transfers and assigns all its right, title and interest, to the designated trademark, application and registration, together with the goodwill of the business in which the mark is used and symbolized, to Assignee.

Any assignment of federal trademark rights must include the goodwill as a recital, or it will be refused recordal. The trademark assignment usually is placed in a separate document for recordal purposes. This way, details of the overall business transaction can be kept confidential.

Other provisions frequently included in an assignment are:

(1) a recital confirming that the transfer was made for good and valuable consideration;

(2) a statement of the geographic territory of the rights assigned;

(3) a list of all pending or registered trademarks included in the assignment;

(4) the right to sue and recover damages for past infringements (If an infringement suit is ongoing, or if oppositions or cancellations are pending, these issues will have to be addressed.); and

(5) the assignee's full name and address.

---

[5] For example, there would not be any problem where the trademark
is owned by a corporation and all the corporate stock is sold.

[6] §10

Other matters to consider include: whether the assignor has any trademarked material with its name or logo which should be disposed of or destroyed; whether there is any inventory of product which should be transferred; whether any foreign rights are to be transferred and whether the assignment is subject to any consent agreements or licenses.

Trademark assignments are unilateral so that only the assignor needs to sign. Acknowledgment is prima facie evidence of the execution of the assignment.

RECORDAL OF ASSIGNMENTS

It is important for the assignee to promptly record the assignment with the U.S. Patent and Trademark Office to preclude assignment to a subsequent purchaser without notice and for valuable consideration. Also, having title will allow the assignee to take actions as necessary to maintain the registration, or to prosecute an application. Once the recordal is filed, the registration will be presumed valid and owned by the assignee. A sample trademark assignment form which can be used for recordal with the Trademark Office is included in the Addendum to this chapter.

Normally, it is the duty of the assignee to record the assignment to make of record its equitable title in the Trademark Office. This requires payment of a fee and submittal of a special recordal cover sheet (Appendix Fourteen) along with the trademark assignment form.

An assignment is void against any subsequent purchaser for valuable consideration without notice, unless it is recorded in the U.S. Patent and Trademark Office within *three months* after the date thereof, or prior to such subsequent purchase. The date of receipt of the assignment by the Patent and Trademark Office will control.

There is no time limit on recording assignments. However, the assignee will have to record the assignment before taking an action concerning the trademark. Where multiple marks are being assigned, generally they can be included in a single application, since the goodwill can be assigned without earmarking.

Can a trademark owner assign trademark rights to part of the goods listed in a registration and keep the remainder or assign rights to one class and keep another? The owner cannot split a registration, and there are no registration reissue procedures.[7]

RECORDING ASSIGNMENTS

A trademark registration or application and common law rights for a mark are assigned to you. What is the next step? Since official title for applications and registrations is kept in the Patent and Trademark Office, you need to correct title to your name so that you can prosecute the case, renew the registration and make a subsequent assignment.

Each recordal must be accompanied by a special cover sheet and an appropriate fee. The Patent and Trademark Office does not determine the validity of the assignments, and conditional assignments are treated as absolute. The common law assignment is superfluous, but is recorded if it is part of the overall transaction.

A trademark registration can be issued to the assignee upon written request if assignment or name change documents have been recorded. The certificate can be reissued upon payment of an additional fee.

ASSIGNMENT FEE

The current assignment recordal fee is $40 (includes one mark). Additional marks in the same assignment are $25 each. If the assignee wants a new certificate of registration, it will cost $50 for each registration.

ASSIGNMENT AND GRANT BACK

A grant back refers to the situation where an assignment of a trademark is made, and the assignee grants a license back to the original grantor. This usually comes into play where the original owner wants to continue to sell products on a limited scale.

---

[7] In retrospect, the party should have obtained multiple registrations, since they can be separately assigned.

PERSONAL NAMES

Problems often occur when marks which are personal names are assigned. The individual normally will not be willing to change his or her legal name. Typically, in these types of transfers, the assignor will enter into a non-compete agreement which is valid for a certain amount of time. When that time period expires, the assignor will frequently start up a new company.

Consider the following example. Dippy Smith has a catfish restaurant business, operating under the service mark "DIPPY SMITH." That business and service mark is subsequently sold. After his non-competition clause has expired, Dippy decides to open a restaurant which features carry-out fast food in a different area of town. The new restaurant is operated under the name and mark "DIPPY'S." The most distinctive portion of the mark has been appropriated. In this situation, the court is likely to approve a settlement whereby Dippy Smith agrees to have notations in his advertising and at his new business location stating that he is not associated with the original DIPPY SMITH restaurant.

There is no inherent right to use a name in business and the owner is always subject to priority rights of other parties.

ASSIGNMENT OF LITERARY TITLES

Literary titles and their assignment present special problems.[8] Titles to periodicals or a series of works can be registered in Int. Class 16. However, titles of unitary literary works are considered generic or descriptive and require proof of secondary meaning. Goodwill problems may develop where a title is purchased and used apart from the copyrighted work. An example is where a novel is sold to Hollywood, and the title, but little else, is used for the movie. This happens a lot.[9]

Can the title be protected separately from the work? This is equivalent to separating a trademark from its goodwill, which cannot legally be done. Another area where caution should be

---

[8] Titles are not copyrighted. They are not trademarks either since they are generic of the product.

[9] The James Bond movie "Casino Royal" comes to mind.

exercised is where spin-off trademark merchandising rights to a mark are being sold independently of the underlying work.

CONSIDERATION AND PAYMENT

There is no requirement that the assignor be paid anything for an assignment. A recitation of nominal consideration is understood as just that and is ignored. However, to be safe, any contract to assign should be supported by actual consideration.

CHAIN OF TITLE

The assignor is responsible for passing title to the assignee and should, at assignor's cost, correct the chain of title to show ownership in the assignor.[10] If the assignor has undergone a change in corporate structure, the assignor will have to correct the chain of title *before* an assignment can be recorded. In this situation, the assignee can use merger and change of name documentation for recordal purposes or effect another assignment from the old company to the new. It is important not to skip any steps since goodwill will have to be tacked.

SECURITY INTERESTS

Trademarks can be pledged as security for a debt. Under one procedure, a conditional or collateral assignment is used to transfer title to the creditor with a license back to the assignor. This does not require the transfer of goodwill because this is only a *conditional* promise to make a future assignment. Another procedure is to give the creditor a lien on the trademark and assets, coupled with a power of attorney to assign the mark in the event of a default.

Trademarks are classified as "general intangibles" under the Uniform Commercial Code (UCC). In order to be valid against third parties, recordal of state or common law trademarks should be made by filing a finance statement in accordance with UCC requirements in the state where the debtor is located. It has been

---

[10] Frequently, title to older registrations will be in some predecessor company.

argued that UCC recordal is unnecessary if recordal of the security interest is made with the Patent and Trademark Office. However, in the case *In re Roman Cleaner*, 43. B.R. 940, *aff'd*, 802 F2d 207 (6th Cir. 1984), the court held that a security interest is not a presently operating assignment and falls under UCC control. The safest procedure is to record both ways.

BANKRUPTCY

Trademarks are part of the estate of an insolvent and can be assigned for the benefit of creditors with the goodwill of the business. *It does no good to put in a clause reciting that an agreement can be terminated in the event of bankruptcy, since termination of contracts under bankruptcy proceedings is controlled by federal law.*

FOREIGN TRADEMARKS

Where there is a transfer involving foreign trademarks, there will be an agreement assigning the marks. This puts equitable assignment in the assignee. For formal assignment, documents have to be prepared and filed case-by-case and country-by-country. This is almost as expensive as filing a new trademark application. The assignee normally bears all recordal costs, except that the assignor customarily makes any recordals necessary to bring his title up to date.

CROSS REFERENCES

See Chapter Twelve covering licenses. The Addendum to this chapter has an assignment form.

ADDENDUM: TRADEMARK ASSIGNMENT FORM

WHEREAS, _____ , a corporation of _____, whose business address is _____, ("Assignor"), is the owner of the trademark, application and registration set forth below:

Mark   Ser. No.   Appln. Date   Reg. No.   Reg. Date

(hereinafter "the Mark")

WHEREAS, _____ , a corporation of _____, whose business address is _____,(Assignee"), desires to acquire rights and title to the Mark and said application and registration;

THEREFORE, for good and valuable consideration, Assignor assigns, sets over, transfers all of Assignor's rights, titles and interests to the Mark, application and registration, including rights of goodwill in connection with the business with which the Mark is used or symbolized, to Assignee.

Assignor

By: _____

_____

Date

ASSIGNMENT COVER LETTER

The Patent and Trademark Office requires that any assignment submitted for recordal be filed with a mandatory cover sheet containing background information and data. This form, which is included in Appendix Fourteen, should always accompany the trademark assignment form.

Twelve

Licensing

Because of limited resources, manufacturing equipment and marketing means, many trademark owners decide to license their trademark rights to third party manufacturers or service providers. Trademark licensing affords opportunities to both the licensor (trademark owner) and licensee (manufacturer or service provider). The licensor expands his market without incurring too many costs and receives royalties in the process. The licensee is able to market new products or provide services under the licensor's trademarks.

Historically, trademark licensing was prohibited, because it resulted in multiple manufacturers and sources behind a product, which was considered contrary to the purpose of a trademark — to designate source. The perception was that by not producing the product or performing the service directly, the trademark owner was deceiving the public. When the perception of quality control shifted from the manufacture of the goods to the quality of the products, the way was cleared for the trademark owner to license.

Under the concept of the owner exercising quality control over the goods, it was accepted that licensing was not an abandonment of the trademark. However, for a long time, sublicensing remained suspect because the licensor lost direct control.[1] Service marks had even a longer way to come, since they were not recognized at common law, much less be subject to licenses or sublicenses.

Licensing takes many forms. The licensor or trademark owner can grant royalty-bearing licenses to franchisees and others. The licensor can give permissions or consents to other parties to register. The licensor can have trading name agreements between a parent and its subsidiaries and affiliates. Licenses are

---

[1] In Taiwan, there is still a prohibition against sublicensing.

frequently granted to vendors who produce various merchandise items with company names or logos.

Licenses can be exclusive, non-exclusive, oral, written, or implied. They can be stand-alone agreements or be included as provisions in other agreements. They can be territorially restricted, time-restricted or restricted as to goods and services.

LICENSING AND INTENT TO USE

Intent to use dovetails perfectly with licensing. Previously the product or service had to be sold or provided in interstate commerce before a trademark or service mark could be applied for. Not so any more. Now an applicant can apply based on an intent to use and meet the use requirement by licensing. Therefore, the entrepreneur can develop a name or mark for a product or service, and have a licensee make the sales or provide the services, provided that quality control is maintained.

BASIC ELEMENTS OF A TRADEMARK LICENSE

Licensing is similar for all kinds of intellectual property rights, technologies and goods. Whether you are dealing with geophysical exploration, petrochemical plants, convenience stores, airplanes, characters, etc., the property owner is licensing intellectual property rights and support services of some type. Stripped to their essentials, licenses are consents, plus know-how or assistance. The licensor tells a manufacturer he can make something using the licensor's trademark, and the licensor gives him a consent. Add to it the know-how or assistance, and you have a license.

But trademarks also have some special requirements. To maintain the concept of a single source, a trademark license must: (1) indicate that rights flow back to (inure to) the licensor and (2) explicitly show that the licensor is exercising quality control. If either of these two requirements is not met, the trademark owner's rights may be ruled abandoned and lost. As a result, the quality control provisions in a trademark license agreement are extremely important and should be drafted carefully.

Otherwise, a trademark license is handled much like any other license agreement. The licensor sets policy regarding the term of the agreement, royalties, confidentiality, indemnification, warranties, training, controlling law, etc. A form trademark license is included in Addendum One to this chapter.

Quality control involves setting specifications and standards and conducting follow-up inspections on the goods being sold, or services being performed, and checking on customer complaints. What works best is actual "hands-on" control, since this confirms that there is a unitary source.

QUALITY CONTROL AGENTS

Can a licensor assign the job of quality control to a third party? This is accepted practice so long as standards are specified and actual control is exercised. For licensees in remote parts of the country, this is a practical and natural arrangement. The licensor should have a written agreement with the agent and maintain evidence to show that inspections were made. The key isn't so much who does the quality control, as that it is done, and that the benefit accrues to the licensor.

In order to satisfy the examiner that use by a licensee inures to the licensor's benefit, quality control support language should be put in every trademark license. This is something the examiner can see and read.[2] This shows an awareness of trademarks and allows the examiner to assume that the arrangement is being handled properly.

Contractual quality control language offers effective window dressing, but "hands on" control by the licensor is what ensures the quality of the products. Without that, the trademark may be deemed abandoned, quality control language in the license notwithstanding. If the licensor engages in naked licensing, i.e., licenses the trademark without providing goodwill, the trademark is put at risk and may be deemed to be abandoned.

It was previously suspect whether a trademark owner could bootstrap himself into acquiring trademark usage rights by

---

[2] Having both contractual language and hands-on quality control works the best.

claiming the first use by a licensee. This issue, however, appears to be resolved:

> If the first use of a mark by a person is controlled by the registrant or applicant for registration of the mark with respect to the nature and quality of the goods or services, such first use shall inure to the benefit of the registrant or applicant . . . .

The trademark owner has flexibility to make direct sales or rely on the sales of a licensee.

LICENSING CHECKLIST

The following is a check list of items that may be present in a trademark license:
1. Identity of the parties
2. The trademark and goods or services
3. The territory
4. The term
5. Quality control provisions
6. Inspection rights
7. Exclusive or non-exclusive license
8. License grant
9. Sublicense rights
10. Trademark acknowledgments
11. Trademark use requirements
12. Termination rights
13. Indemnification of Licensor
14. Royalties
15. Payment
16. Accounting
17. Audit
18. Entire Agreement
19. Infringement
20. Transferability
21. Notice
22. Applicable Law

LICENSING AMONG RELATED COMPANIES

A "related company" is defined in the Lanham Act to mean:[3] ". . . any person whose use of a mark is controlled by the owner of the mark with respect to the nature and quality of the goods or services on or in connection with which the mark is used." Section 5 of the Lanham Act provides a basis for licensing under the *related company* doctrine:

Where a registered mark or a mark sought to be registered is or may be used legitimately by a related company, such use shall inure to the benefit of the registrant or applicant for registration and such use shall not effect the validity of such mark or of its registration, provided such mark is not used in a manner as to deceive the public.

This covers wholly-owned subsidiaries where control is exercised through ownership, as well as affiliates and third parties who are granted licenses. Control of a wholly-owned subsidiary is automatic. However, any affiliate which is less than 100 percent owned should be expressly licensed, the same as a third party. If the licensee qualifies as a related company, the trademark control obligations are deemed to be met.

LICENSOR'S LIABILITY

When licensees manufacture and sell products under license, they are responsible for the safety of the product. But the licensors whose trademarks appear on the products may also be held accountable. Plaintiffs' attorneys are always looking to attack the "deep pockets" in product liability cases, and sometimes that is the licensor. Because of the quality control provisions, trademark licensors are often a natural avenue of attack.

Licensors need to have quality control provisions to ensure the validity of the license, but in a product liability suit, this could get a licensor in trouble. Yet, if the licensor does not exercise control, he may be sued for being negligent in making in-

---

[3] §45

spections. This represents a Catch-22 situation for the licensor. The best course for licensors to take is to be careful about who they license and to take their quality control responsibilities seriously, by closely monitoring the products their licensees produce and by eliminating those products which are likely to cause harm to the consumer.

LICENSEE ESTOPPEL

A *patent* licensor cannot require a licensee, as a condition of receiving the license, to agree not to attack the validity of the patent. This rule, which is referred to as *licensee estoppel*, has no application to trademarks. A trademark licensor can have a licensee sign a waiver against attacking the trademark as part of the license.

VENDOR'S AGREEMENTS

Suppose a licensor is confronted by a manufacturer who wants to prepare a gift catalog or wants to have some T-shirts made with the company logo and sell them to employees at the annual picnic. What should the licensor do? If the licensor does not object to the transaction, then he or she needs to have the party sign a vendor's agreement. This is a short-form license which acknowledges that the trademark rights belong to the licensor, protects the trademark and expands the licensor's scope of product coverage. A sample vendor's agreement is found in Addendum Two to this chapter.

TRADING NAME AGREEMENTS

If a company has subsidiaries or affiliates that use its name, these should be separately licensed even if the party has signed a trademark license agreement. A trading name agreement covers use of the company name or logo by a related company. An example of a trading name agreement is found in Addendum Three to this chapter.

CONSENT AGREEMENTS

Consent agreements are special forms of licenses where one party is granting the other a consent to register.[4] It used to be that consents weren't generally accepted by the U.S. Patent and Trademark Office, but a line of cases has concluded that the parties know the market best and therefore, have approved them. The parties may enter into a collateral agreement defining how their marks will be used, or the party granting the consent may require a collateral undertaking safeguarding his rights.[5]

FRANCHISING

Franchising is a trademark licensing system where the licensee is required to pay a certain amount of front-end money the first six months and where both the licensor and licensee have duties beyond normal trademark duties. The Federal Government and state governments have all passed franchise or business opportunity regulations. (See Chapter Thirteen.)

LICENSES AND ASSIGNMENTS DISTINGUISHED

An assignment is a transfer or sale of title where the licensor disposes of all its rights to a property.[6] A license is a grant of something lesser. Part of the bundle of trademark owner's rights are granted to another party, but the owner still has some of the rights left.[7] The licensor agrees not to sue the licensee during the term of the agreement, if the licensee performs within the

---

[4] Usually there are no royalties, but sometimes the party granting the consent will ask that his expenses be covered.

[5] These agreements can either be limited to a particular country or be global.

[6] When is a sale not a sale? Whenever it involves a copyright interest. Under the termination of grant provisions, at approximately the mid-point in the term of copyright, the original copyright owner can give a notice of termination and take title or whatever grant was made back. There is no such boomerang effect with trademarks.

[7] Often the same result can be achieved if an assignment is made and the assignee grants a license back to the assignor.

scope of the grant. If the license is exclusive, the licensor has covenanted not to license anyone else.

The Lanham Act requires that federally registered marks and trademark applications be assigned in writing. (See Chapter Eleven.) There are no statutory requirements relating to licenses. Normally, both parties will want to have any licenses put in writing so that they can be recorded. The trademark owner also needs to be alert for situations where another party could allege that a license has been granted by implication.[8] If the licensor only grants licenses in writing, this may help prove that an implied license has not been granted.

CROSS REFERENCES

See Chapter Thirteen on franchise agreements. The Addendums to this chapter include forms for a trademark license, a vendor's agreement and a trading name agreement.

---

[8] Sending confirming letters stating your case after phone calls with potential licensees or infringers is a good way to defuse future conflicts.

ADDENDUM ONE:
TRADEMARK LICENSE AGREEMENT (NON-EXCLUSIVE)

AGREEMENT made this ___ day of ____, 199__, by and between _____ ("LICENSOR") and _____ ("LICENSEE");

Whereas, LICENSOR owns or has licensing rights to certain trademarks, logos, and designs ("the Trademark");

Whereas, LICENSEE desires to use the Trademark to sell and distribute the goods designated in Appendix A hereto ("the Goods"); and

Now, therefore, for and in consideration of the premises, it is agreed by the parties as follows:

I. LICENSE GRANT

1.1 Subject to the terms and conditions set forth herein, LICENSOR grants to LICENSEE a non-exclusive royalty-bearing license to use the Trademark for the sale and distribution of the Goods in the United States.

1.2 The Goods shall be selected in accordance with LICENSOR's specifications and standards, or otherwise approved as to quality by LICENSOR. LICENSEE shall allow LICENSOR upon request to inspect or obtain samples of the Goods.

1.3 The Trademark shall be used or applied to the Goods in accordance with LICENSOR's design standards. LICENSOR reserves the right to review and approve all labeling and packaging involving the Trademark.

1.4 All rights of usage of the Trademark shall inure to the benefit of LICENSOR and be the property of LICENSOR, and LICENSEE agrees not to register the Trademark as a trademark, or use or register same as a trade name.

II. ROYALTIES AND REPORTS

2.1 LICENSEE agrees to pay LICENSOR fees of ___ percent

of the "Net Sales" of the Goods. By "Net Sales" is meant gross sales and revenues received by LICENSEE for sales and distribution of the Goods, less transportation charges, sales taxes and returns.

2.2 All payments required by LICENSEE hereunder shall be made within 60 days after the end of each calendar quarter to LICENSOR or LICENSOR's or designated bank. Each payment will include a written report showing the Net Sales for the period and how they were calculated.

2.3 LICENSOR shall have the right to audit LICENSEE's books and records pertaining to the sales and distribution of the Goods.

III. TERM AND TERMINATION

3.1 The term of this Agreement shall be for ___ months, starting _____ and ending _____ . After termination, LICENSEE shall pay LICENSOR any royalties which accrued during the term of the Agreement.

3.2 All materials bearing the Trademark which LICENSEE has in its possession shall be disposed of according to LICENSOR's directions.

IV. ASSIGNMENT

4.1 This Agreement is personal to LICENSEE, and cannot be assigned or sublicensed without LICENSOR's written permission. LICENSOR has the right to assign the Agreement to a purchaser or beneficiary of its business or goodwill to which the Trademark pertains.

V. GENERAL

5.1 Notices shall be given by the parties to each other at the addresses first above given unless otherwise specified in writing. Notices may be given by E-mail or fax, if confirmed by certified mail, or by an express mail service.

5.2 This Agreement is the entire agreement of the parties pertaining to the subject matter thereof and cannot be amended or modified without the written consent of the other party.

5.3 The laws of the state of _____ shall be used in interpreting this Agreement.

IN WITNESS WHEREOF, the parties have caused this Agreement to be executed by their duly authorized representatives the day and year first above given.

LICENSEE   LICENSOR

By _____   By _____

ADDENDUM TWO: VENDOR'S AGREEMENT

In consideration of being approved by _____ ("OWNER") to produce or mark and sell certain goods ("Goods") with OWNER's trademarks and designs (the "Marks"), _____ ("VENDOR") agrees as follows:

1. All trademark rights to the Marks shall belong exclusively to OWNER.
2. All Goods shall be approved by OWNER and shall be of a quality specified by OWNER.
3. The Marks shall be used in a form approved by OWNER.
4. VENDOR shall never claim any rights to the Marks.
5. VENDOR shall indemnify and defend OWNER from any product liability claims resulting from the Goods or arising out of this Agreement.
6. This Agreement shall terminate after one year. OWNER can terminate upon five days notice to VENDOR upon VENDOR's default.
7. Upon termination, any Goods remaining in inventory shall be disposed of according to OWNER's instructions.
8. These terms cannot be changed except by OWNER's written approval.
9. The rights granted VENDOR cannot be assigned.

Agreement made this __ day of ___, 19__ by:

VENDOR   OWNER

By: _____   By: _____

ADDENDUM THREE: TRADING NAME AGREEMENT

Agreement made as of the ___ day of ___, 19 , by and between _____ ("PARENT") and _____ "SUBSIDIARY");

Whereas, PARENT is the owner of the trademark and name ("the Name") when used as a trademark, service mark, trade name or trading style in the field of activities in which PARENT and its subsidiaries and divisions and units operate or intent to operate; and

Whereas, PARENT has consented to allow SUBSIDIARY to use the Name in SUBSIDIARY's name, subject to the conditions set forth hereafter.

Now, Therefore, PARENT and SUBSIDIARY wish to confirm their agreement as follows:

1. PARENT has granted and hereby grants to SUBSIDIARY the right to use the Name in its corporate name and to register same in a form approved by PARENT.

2. SUBSIDIARY acknowledges that the Name is the property of PARENT and that it will not, unless separately licensed by PARENT, use or register the Name as a trademark.

3. This grant is personal to SUBSIDIARY and cannot be assigned, transferred or used by SUBSIDIARY's subsidiaries or affiliates, except PARENT.

4. SUBSIDIARY reserves the right to cease using the Name upon thirty days prior written notice to PARENT.

5. PARENT reserves the right to terminate in the event of default by SUBSIDIARY, or if PARENT ceases to own directly or indirectly all of SUBSIDIARY's voting stock.

6. Upon termination, SUBSIDIARY's name shall be officially changed to delete the Name, and SUBSIDIARY shall take all

reasonable steps to remove the Name from its facilities, stationery, signage, and from telephone directories, trade journals and the like.

In witness whereof, this agreement is entered into by the parties effective the earlier of the date SUBSIDIARY first legally came into existence, or the Name is used by SUBSIDIARY.

PARENT   SUBSIDIARY

By _____   By _____

Thirteen

Franchising

Franchising is trademark licensing coupled with a substantial business commitment by both the licensor and licensee. Federal and state regulations mandate what information must be disclosed to potential franchisees, require registration by the franchisor and monitor the terms of the franchise agreements. The assumptions are that the franchisee cannot protect himself, and that every franchisor wears a black hat. Consequently, the franchise agreement has become a disclosure document rather than an intellectual property license. The result: government regulation at its epitome and a morass of overlapping paperwork and regulations.

Twenty years ago, trademark licensing in the U.S. was no different than licensing any other form of intellectual property. A licensor and licensee would conclude an agreement covering the use which the licensee wanted to make of the licensor's trademarks, a royalty was negotiated and provision was made for supplying whatever technical assistance and training was required. No disclosure treatises were mandated prior to contracting, the licensor did not register with any authorities and statutory licensing conditions were not imposed on the license. Trademark licensing can still be done like this in foreign countries, and even in the U.S. if the license is not considered a franchise.[1] The good news is that while the highly regulated franchise system used by the U.S. has been around for a while, other coun-

---

[1] Comparing U.S. and foreign licenses for the same franchise, you would think that they are totally unrelated subject matters. The U.S. franchise agreement looks totally different and is primarily a disclosure document. Foreign agreements are just normal licenses.

tries have not rushed to adopt it.[2] The bad news is that most states have adopted franchising or business opportunity laws to supplement the federal regulations.

If a license has enough extra trappings so that it metamorphosizes into a "franchise," the various federal and state regulations kick in. And the parties to a franchise end up with an agreement form whose format is a collection of statistics, names, dates and numbers. A trademark license this is not, since the regulations were put in to satisfy the government and not to commemorate the intentions of the parties involved.

THE DEFINITION OF FRANCHISING

A general definition of franchising is where "franchisees are granted, in return for a franchise fee or other consideration, the right to market the goods and services of the franchisor in accordance with standards and practices and assistance of the franchisor."[3] If "franchise" was changed to "license," this same definition would apply to most trademark licenses. Therefore, something more distinguishing is needed. What additional features are there that identify a franchise?

Franchising is a comprehensive form of licensing where the franchisor provides more assistance than under a license agreement, and the franchisee makes a substantial business commitment to use the trademark. From the franchisors' perspective, franchising provides a means for expanding and increasing income without making a capital investment. Usually private individuals who expect to derive an income from the business are the franchisees. Along with the trademarks which are licensed, usually goes a complete business operation. And the franchisor, who usually has franchised similar operations, provides extensive assistance in the start-up and ongoing operations.

---

[2] Another factor is that most franchising in foreign countries is done with established firms and companies that are very sophisticated when it comes to franchising. However, sublicensing is usually done with small local firms or businesses.

[3] Obviously one shouldn't use the term that is being defined in the definition, but that's what was done.

GOVERNMENT REGULATION

Because most individuals are unsophisticated in complex business and licensing arrangements, the federal and state governments have imposed various controls. The federal government, acting through the Federal Trade Commission (FTC), requires disclosure of certain information to the prospective franchisees. The primary abuses that the laws were aimed at preventing include: (1) unjust terminations by the franchisor; (2) arbitrary refusals by the franchisor to extend or renew the agreement; and (3) refusals by the franchisor to allow franchisees to assign their rights. Additionally, most states have imposed controls on franchises to address these and other problems. Two systems of state control exist: some states regulate the offering and execution of the franchise, while other states give the franchisees special termination and other post-execution rights.

As is the case with state and federal trademarks, the federal and state franchise regulations coexist. Whether a specific transaction is controlled federally, at the state level or concurrently, depends on how the franchise is defined. This means checking the federal requirements and reviewing the state regulations for any state remotely involved in the transaction and comparing them against the proposed operation. Results will vary from state to state.

THE FTC RULE[4]

To further compound matters, two definitions of a *franchise* are used by the FTC:[5] one is a "package and product franchise" and the other is a "business opportunity venture." To be a package and product franchise, three elements must be present: (1) the franchisee must sell goods or services which meet the franchisor's quality standards, or which are identified by the franchisor's mark; (2) the franchisor must exercise control over the operation or provide significant technical assistance; and (3)

---

[4] This became effective in 1979.
[5] The Federal Trade Commission's Trade Regulation Rule, Disclosure Requirements and Prohibitions Concerning Franchises and Business Opportunity Ventures, 16 C.F.R. Part 436.

the franchisee must be required to make payments of $500 or more to the franchisor before or within six months after a business opens.

To be a business opportunity venture, again, three elements are involved: (1) the franchisee must sell goods and services which are supplied by the franchisor or a person affiliated with the franchisor; (2) the franchisor must assist the franchisee in securing accounts for the franchise or securing locations or sites for vending machines or rack displays; and (3) the franchisee must be required to make payments aggregating $500 or more to the franchisor before the business has been open six months.

In either category, if less than $500 is required until after the business has been open for six months, the agreement is outside the FTC Rule. *Therefore, franchisors have an out if they want it — to defer obtaining any funds until after six months.*

FRANCHISE CONTROL PROPOSAL

Rather than dumping on the public more information than they need, a more logical approach would be to establish a national franchise registration system where franchisors would have to register and be renewed annually. The government can ask all the questions and gather whatever information they want. For new franchises, special termination provisions could be required for the first dozen franchisees as a condition of receiving provisional approval. The state controls could be eliminated in total, and the franchise agreements would again be simple licenses which the parties negotiate.

THE FTC GUIDELINES

The FTC Rule is a disclosure-based system. The franchisor must make certain background disclosures to the prospective licensees. An *offering circular* is prepared by the franchisor in a prescribed format, which discloses certain information to the prospective franchisees. This offering circular must be tendered to the franchisee before negotiations and must be updated annually. There is no registration of the franchisors or control of the licensing procedures or contract provisions. Franchise agreements must be written in a prescribed format and be in "plain English."

THE NEW FTC REGULATIONS

The new FTC Regulations now require more information to be disclosed by the franchisor. Now, the franchisor must disclose the following in the offering circular to potential franchisees:

Item 1. The Franchisor, its Predecessors and Affiliates. "Affiliates" is new. Predecessor disclosure is limited to prior ten years.

Item 2. Business experience. The business experience of directors, principal officers, franchise executives and marketing management must be disclosed.

Item 3. Litigation. This item includes litigations involving franchisor and predecessors, as well as parties in Item 2. Administrative actions are included. Disclosure of felony convictions or "no contest" pleas for previous ten years is required.

Item 4. Bankruptcy. Ten year prior disclosure.

Item 5. Initial Franchise Fee. The initial fee must be disclosed and conditions stated as to when it is refundable.

Item 6. Other Fees. All other fees must be disclosed in a tabular form. This is where royalties come in.

Item 7. Initial Investment. Payments and all costs necessary to operate a business during its initial phase must be disclosed.

Item 8. Restrictions on Sources of Products and Services. This item requires listing the goods required to be purchased from the franchisor, its designate, suppliers or purchased under the franchisor's specifications.

Item 9. Franchisee's Obligations. This is new. Disclosure must be made in tabular form. There are twenty-five categories.

Item 10. Financing. Direct and indirect financing offered by the franchisor and its affiliates must be disclosed.

Item 11. Franchisor's Obligations. This includes training and technical assistance. Also, advertising fits in here.

Item 12. Territory. Information must be disclosed concerning alternative channels of distribution using the franchisor's trademark.

Item 13. Trademarks. Disclosure is now in chart form, and a fair amount of detailed information must be given. However, it would take a trademark attorney to understand much of it. Only the principal trademarks require disclosure, and disclosure can be limited to the states where the franchises are offered. Intent to use applications must be identified. If the principal trademark is not registered on the Principal Register, a warning is required.

Item 14. Patents, Copyrights, and Proprietary Information. Confidential information should be identified and the terms and conditions of its use specified. In other words, the know-how and business and technical information have finally been included.[6]

Item 15. Obligation to Participate in the Actual Operation of the Franchise Business. This covers all obligations placed on the franchisee's manager.

Item 16. Restrictions on What the Franchisee May Sell. The document must specify whether the franchisor can change goods and services sold or provided by the franchisee.

Item 17. Renewal, Termination, Transfer, and Dispute Resolution. All of these topics are important enough to be separate categories. Obligations must be set forth in chart form. This is extremely detailed.

Item 18. Public Figures.

Item 19. Earnings Claim.

Item 20. List of Outlets. Chart form required; covers outlets over the last three years.

Item 21. Financial Statements. Franchisor must include balance sheets for the previous two years.

Item 22. Contracts.

Item 23. Receipt. The offering circular must include a de-

---

[6] They still don't understand copyrights. They talk about listing the copyrights — copyrights are automatic and everything being conveyed is copyrighted. How can anyone make a complete list of copyrights? And copyright renewals are, for the most part, history.

tachable sheet with various information items to be filled out confirming that proper advance distribution was made.

The new guidelines (and the old guidelines too for that matter) are unduly complex and difficult to understand and use. And the franchisor is forced to incur needless legal and accounting fees. While some franchisees may be protected, it puts a damper on the franchising process overall, and all the costs eventually are footed by the public.[7]

STATE REGULATIONS

Now for the other half of the story. State franchise or business opportunity regulations concurrently exist with the federal regulations and may be applicable, even if the agreement is outside the scope of the FTC Rule. The state definitions of franchising differ from the federal definitions and from one another. Some states use franchising regulations to raise money. The need for regulation is just an excuse. Other states have reasonable fees and regulate franchises in order to protect their citizens. Two types of state regulation systems have developed: (1) those that regulate the offer and sale of franchises and (2) business opportunity statutes that control the post-sale franchise.

Some aspects of an agreement that the state laws typically cover include: (1) discrimination against franchisees; (2) arbitration outside the franchisee's state; (3) encroachment on the franchisee's territory; (4) free association among the franchisees; (5) requirements for good cause for termination; (6) the term of agreements and renewals, (7) transfers by assignment and by operation of law; and (8) injunctive relief, damages and repurchase.

---

[7] The above was programmed by financial experts who know and care little about normal procedures of business or licensing and have never operated their own business. For example, the most important part of any license, the "license grant," isn't apparent. Somewhere along the way the government started compiling financial data and information rather than concerning themselves with disclosures that would supplement the provisions in a conventional license. Most of the up-front information the government requires would be buried in an Appendix in a standard license, if included at all. It simply is not of interest and is not part of any decision-making process.

There are about fifteen states that have franchise controls and close to twenty-five states that have business opportunity statutes. Some states have both. California and New York are examples of franchise control states and Texas, Alabama and California are business opportunity states. (California is an example of a state that swings both ways.)

Fees are not insubstantial and generally are periodical. Besides a registration fee, there may be renewal fees, amendment fees and even exemption fees.[8] Depending on the location of the franchisor and franchisee and where the franchise will be, it may be necessary to qualify in several states. Thus, it may be necessary to obtain opinions from attorneys and even incur fees in each of the states in question.

SPECIAL FEDERAL FRANCHISE STATUTES

In addition to the FTC Rule which covers franchises in general, there are government regulations which cover various specific industries or businesses. Examples include the Petroleum Marketing Practices Act (PMPA) dealing with gasoline station franchises and The Automobile Dealer's Day in Court Act. The former receives a lot of action, while the latter has been little used.

The states are substantive players in the franchise regulatory scheme. It is the duty of the franchisor and franchisee to determine which states will be affected and to review their current franchising provisions. The state laws control the relationships of the parties, which is something the FTC has never done.

CONCLUSION

When franchising first started, protective laws were needed. The public was unsophisticated, and the licensors did not know what they were doing either. But that time has passed, and the

---

[8] The fees frequently increase and have not been shown. Typically, initial franchise fees will range between $500 and 1000. Renewal fees are between $250 and $500. Business opportunity fees are usually less.

regulations should be eased back. The government's role as a midwife is finished. The governments should let the parties negotiate the style of agreement they want. A franchise will only work if its good for both parties, and the market, not government laws and regulations, should determine which franchises survive or fail.

CROSS REFERENCES

See Chapter Twelve on licensing and Chapter Fourteen on state trademarks. The Addendum to this chapter is a commentary on state business opportunity and franchise statutes.

ADDENDUM ONE: STATE FRANCHISE LAWS

The following is a summary of state franchise and business opportunity regulations. Definitions of franchises vary. The laws and fees change regularly; local phone numbers are provided for follow-up.

ALABAMA
No business opportunity or franchise statutes.

ALASKA
No business opportunity or franchise statutes.

ARIZONA
No business opportunity or franchise statutes.

ARKANSAS
– *Franchise law,* but there are no filing or disclosure requirements. No fees. It is unlawful to defraud or fail to disclose material facts. The state has franchise termination control provisions. Securities Commissioner, Little Rock, 501-682-3405.

CALIFORNIA
– *Franchise law;* registration and annual renewal. Registration fee currently is $450. Commissioner of Corporations, 213-736-2741; Sacramento, 916-445-7205; San Francisco, 415-557-3787.
– *Bus. Opt. law;* registration and annual renewal. San Diego, 415-557-3787.

COLORADO
No franchise or business opportunity laws.

CONNECTICUT
– *Bus. Opt. law;* annual renewal. Fee is $400. There is an exemption for federally registered trademarks. Commissioner of Banking, Hartford, 302-566-4560.

DELAWARE
There are no franchise sales statutes.
– *Bus. Opt. law;* regulates termination and non-renewal of franchises. Dover, 302-736-3073.

DISTRICT OF COLUMBIA
No franchising or business opportunity statues.

FLORIDA
– *Bus. Opt. law;* annual renewal. Consumer Services, Tallahassee, 904-488-2221.

GEORGIA
– *Bus. Opt. law;* no fees. Check with city and county.

HAWAII
– *Franchise law;* annual renewal. Commerce and Consumer Affairs, Honolulu, 808-548-2021.

IDAHO
No franchising or business opportunity statutes.

ILLINOIS
– *Franchise law;* annual renewal. Franchise Div., Springfield, 217-782-4465.

INDIANA
– *Franchise law;* annual renewal. Franchise Sect., Indiana Securities Div., Indianapolis, 317-232-6257.
– *Bus. Opt. law;* annual renewal. Consumer Affairs, Indianapolis, 317-232-6681.

IOWA
– *Bus. Opt. law;* annual renewal. Insurance Div., Des Moines, 515-281-4441

KANSAS
No general franchise laws.

KENTUCKY
– *Bus. Opt. law*; no fees. Consumer Protection Div., Frankfort, 502-564-2200.

LOUISIANA
– *Bus. Opt. law*; bond required and appointment of Secretary of State as agent for service. Secretary of State, Baton Rouge, 504-925-4698.

MAINE
– *Bus. Opt. law*; annual renewal. State Securities Div., Augustus, 207-582-8760.

MARYLAND
– *Franchise law*; annual renewal. Div. of Securities, Baltimore, 301-576-6360
– *Bus. Opt. law*; annual renewal. Administrator: Same as above.

MASSACHUSETTS
No general statutes governing the sale of franchises or business opportunities.

MICHIGAN
– *Franchise law*; annual renewal. Consumer Protection Div., Lansing, 517-373-7177.

MINNESOTA
– *Franchise law*; annual renewal. Franchise Examiner, St. Paul, 612-296-6328.

MISSISSIPPI
– *Bus. Opt. law*; franchisor can not cancel without 90 days notice and must repurchase inventory. Secretary of State, Jackson, 601-359-1350.

MISSOURI
– *Bus. Opt. law*; 90 days notice by franchisor to cancel; Secretary of State, Jefferson City, 314-751-4756.

MONTANA
No franchising or business opportunity statutes.

NEBRASKA
– *Seller Assisted Marketing Plan.* Depart. Ed. & Financing, Lincoln, 402-471-2171.

NEVADA
No franchising laws.

NEW HAMPSHIRE
– *Bus. Opt. law.* Consumer Protection, Concord, 603-271-3641.

NEW JERSEY
– *Bus. Opt. law*; termination control. Secretary of State, Trenton.

NEW MEXICO
- *Bus. Opt. law*; return of inventory. Secretary of State, Santa Fe, 505-827-3600.

NEW YORK
–*Franchise law*; annual renewal. Investor Protection, New York, 212-416-8816.

NORTH CAROLINA
– *Bus. Opt. law*; annual renewal. Secretary of State, Raleigh, 919-733-3924

NORTH DAKOTA
– *Franchise law*; annual renewal. Franchise Examiner, Bismarck, 710-224-4712.

OHIO
–*Bus. Opt. law*; no term. Consumer Protection, Columbus, 614-466-4910.

OKLAHOMA
– *Bus. Opt. law*; annual renewal. Depart. of Securities, Oklahoma City, 405-235-0230.

OREGON
– *Bus. Opt. law*; annual term. Corporate Securities, Salem, 503-378-4387.

PENNSYLVANIA
No general franchise statutes.

RHODE ISLAND
– *Franchise law*; annual term. Securities Examiner, Providence, 401-277-3048.

SOUTH CAROLINA
– *Bus. Opt. law*; annual renewal. Secretary of State, Columbia, 803-734-2166.

SOUTH DAKOTA
– *Franchise law*; annual term. Securities Div., Pierre, 605-773-4013.

– *Bus. Opt. law*; annual renewal. Contact — see above.

TENNESSEE
No general franchise or business opportunity statutes.

TEXAS
– *Bus. Opt. law*; irregular term. Statutory Document Section, Austin, Texas, 512-475-1769.

UTAH
– *Bus. Opt. law*; no fees or conditions. Depart. of Commerce, Salt Lake City, 801-530-6601.

VERMONT
No general franchise statutes.

VIRGINIA
– *Franchise law*; annual renewal. State Corp. Comm., Richmond, 804-371-9051.

WASHINGTON
– *Franchise law*; annual renewal. Securities Administrator, Olympia, 206-753-6928.

– *Bus. Opt. law*; annual renewal. Administrator same as above.

WEST VIRGINIA
No general franchise statutes.

WISCONSIN
– *Franchise law*; annual renewal. Securities Comm., Madison, 606-266-8559.

WYOMING
No franchising laws.

Fourteen

State Trademarks

The Lanham Act proved so successful that state trademarks are little used or needed today. The reasons are apparent. State trademark rights are typically inadequate. Owners generally want territorial rights. With a federal registration, the owner can preempt the same or similar mark from being used in the entire United States. State registrations, with a few exceptions, do not even preempt the state.

The trademark owner is seeking presumptions of ownership and validity, and most states don't have any meaningful presumptions which attach to their registrations. Trademark owners would like for a registration to become incontestable, and state registrations remain subject to attack for descriptiveness or prior use.

However, state registrations are not without positives:
- they are inexpensive (usually cost less than $50);
- the states provide applications forms which are easy to complete;
- no formal drawings are required;
- the state will usually conduct a pre-application search;
- they are issued quickly;
- they are not subject to a scrutinous examination;
- there are no opposition proceedings; and
- in some states, the applicant can register trade names the same as trademarks.

If an applicant files an application with the state the required number of specimens, and submits the proper fee (usually nominal), generally a trademark registration certificate will issue. Not a bad deal, right? The problem is that the state registrant usually does not get much in the way of added value, and the rights that the registrant does get may not be worth much.

As a rule of thumb, with a state registration, the trademark owner has about the same rights as at common law.[1] And since the owner's common law rights still are intact, the owner has not enhanced his position. All that the owner has done is obtain a registration certificate, for whatever worth or trouble that may be.

Nevertheless, there are collateral aspects of the state trademark laws that are important. Until recently, only states had anti-dilution statutes. These statutes allow owners of famous marks to bring actions where there is no likelihood of confusion.[2]

DILUTION

Trademarks and service marks can be adversely affected by the registration of marks which are identical, even though the goods or services are different. If there are marks with identical names, registered by other sources and for other classes, the original mark has been diluted, and it will have lesser value.

State and federal anti-dilution statutes provide causes of action for likelihood of injury to business reputation or dilution of a distinctive mark or trade name acquired at common law or trademark registered with the state. Likelihood of confusion or competition between the parties is unnecessary.

Another area where the states are still ahead and are likely to remain so is the recordal. The states have statutes for approving and recording corporate and partnership names and dba's. And some states are on the cutting edge in allowing for the registration of trade names the same as trademarks and service marks. The states usually have trademark counterfeiting laws and false advertising laws. However, since now there are federal trademark counterfeiting laws, and Section 43(a) of the Lanham Act protects against false advertising, the state acts have

---

[1] With state registrations, the applicant does not normally get territorial preemption, incontestability or statutory notice.

[2] Federal anti-dilution legislation was only passed in 1996; conversely, a number of states have had anti-dilution statutes for years.

lesser importance. Also, many states have laws which supplement and enhance the federal franchising law. (See Chapter Thirteen.)

THE MODEL TRADEMARK ACT

Most state laws are based on the Model Trademark Act. The Model State Trademark was drafted in 1949 and modeled after the Lanham Act. More than 45 states have adopted legislation based on it. Usually, a state will make a few changes, and since the Model Act has been amended, there are a lot of variations in state trademark laws.

Generally, the requirements for a state trademark under the Model Act are the same as their federal counterpart. To obtain a registration, the applicant usually has to show use (which is interpreted as local use). However, a few states have followed the lead of federal government and adopted an intent to use filing system.

CLASSIFICATION

Originally, the former U.S. classification system was specified. Now the International classification system is the norm. However, some states have been slow to convert.

APPLICATION FOR REGISTRATION

A state application is usually submitted using an official state form. It should be accompanied with three specimens (up from one). However, no drawing or header sheet is required as with a U.S. application. The mark and the goods and services are specified. Also, the date of first use in the state and the date of first use anywhere are requested. The filing fee is usually only a fraction of the U.S. filing fee. The application should include a statement that the applicant is the owner of the mark and that no other person has a right to use the mark in a manner that might deceive or to be mistaken therefor.[3]

---

[3] This statement varies from state to state. It is best to use the official state form.

SEARCHING

Most states will assist in searching. Anyone can call the state office and give them the name of a trademark, and they will search it. This way, trademark owners will know in advance whether they will be able to obtain a registration.

EXAMINATION

For federal applications, federal and state registrations, common law marks and trade names are references. For state trademarks, other state trademarks in that state and common law marks or trade names in that state are considered as references. Usually precluded from consideration are federal registrations and those of other states.[4] When the application is examined, it is either accepted or rejected. The applicant usually does not have an opportunity to offer any input.[5]

CERTIFICATE OF REGISTRATION

The certificate of registration shows the owner, the mark, the class, the goods or services, the registration date and the term of the registration. It is admissible into evidence in court, but usually there is no presumption of validity or right to use.[6]

DURATION AND RENEWAL

State trademarks are usually valid for ten years from registration and are usually renewable for like terms. Submission of

---

[4] This has resulted in an imbalance in the trademark laws. State trademarks are references against federal applications, but federal registration does not bar state registration. Therefore, state trademarks are granted that infringe federal marks.

[5] This may be changed in the future. It would be more efficient than having the applicant refile every time a question or rejection arose.

[6] Sometimes, state registrants will have statutory remedies that they didn't have at common law. But these pale in comparison to those offered under the Lanham Act.

a standard renewal form and payment of a fee are normally required. The state is supposed to notify the applicant before the renewal is due.[7]

ASSIGNMENTS

A mark and its goodwill are assignable with the business with which it is used. Assignments must be by written instruments. A recordal fee is required, and some states have official assignment forms that must be used.

There is a three-month grace period for recordal.[8] Having a state trademark is in a sense a complication, since the applicant will have to be concerned about compliance with assignment and other formalities.[9]

STATE LICENSES

No provision is made for licenses under the Model State Trademark Act. This means licenses can be oral or written and that there are no recordal provisions. It also means that licenses are not officially sanctioned. And because there are no state license provisions, there is no presumption of control by the parent which exists at the federal level.

CANCELLATION

Oppositions are not permitted. However, the Model Act provides several ways to cancel a state registration, although this is often easier said than done, and usually a court determination is required. Therefore, a party wishing to cancel a registration must go to the expense of bringing a court action to show aban-

---

[7] This is not something the applicant should rely on.

[8] If recordal is not made in time, a good faith purchaser without notice can intervene.

[9] Since the owner normally assigns common law rights and goodwill with the federal marks, the owner's tank may already be empty when assigning the state registrations. This problem can be avoided by using a single instrument, but for recordal purposes, the owner would like to have them kept separate.

donment or must show that the registrant is not the owner or that the registration was improperly granted or fraudulently obtained.[10]

Getting bogus registrations nullified should be easy, but often that is not the case. Some parties file state trademarks on famous marks and then license manufacturers to make collector models and other collateral products. When the trademark owner finds out, it is often difficult to deal with the situation, since the Secretary of State usually has no basis for removing the registration.

PROPOSED REVISIONS TO THE MODEL ACT

It has been proposed that the applicant should identify any identical federal registration that he or she has and disclose if the application was rejected by the U.S. Patent and Trademark Office. Another proposal is that states examine applications and interact with the applicant. The term is proposed to be reduced to *five* years.

CROSS REFERENCES

See Chapter Seventeen on litigation and Chapter Thirteen on Franchising.

---

[10] If the other party cannot be located for service, the registrant has real problems.

ADDENDUM ONE:
SUMMARY OF STATE TRADEMARK LAWS
(Further information is available by calling the
Secretaries of State.)

ALABAMA
Trademarks, service marks and trade names are registrable. Local use is required. The state will conduct a search. Actions can be based on dilution or injury to business reputation. There is no intent to use. Corporate names are not references. The term is ten years. Renewal forms are available. There are no presumptions of ownership. Secretary of State, Montgomery, 205-242-5325 or 202-242-7200.

ALASKA
Only trademarks are protected. The application and renewal fees are $10.00. The term is ten years. There are no dilution statutes or intent to use applications. 907-465-3520.

ARIZONA
Trademarks are registrable, but service marks are not. Local use is required for registration. Trade names are only registrable as fictitious names. Renewal and assignment forms are available. There is no dilution statute or intent to use. The state will conduct a search. No statutory presumptions exist. Secretary of State, Phoenix, 602-542-6178 or 602-542-3012.

ARKANSAS
Trademarks and service marks can be registered. Local use is required. A mark cannot be registered if it is registered by another with the U.S. Patent and Trademark Office.[11] The state will conduct searches. Renewal notices are not given, and use does not have to be alleged to maintain a registration. Terms are five years. Renewal forms are provided by the state. No statutory presumptions exist. The state has a dilution statute. Secretary of State, Little Rock, 501-682-3405 or 501-682-1010.

---

[11] This is a very positive step. More states should follow suit.

CALIFORNIA

State-provided application and renewal forms are available. Classification is based on the U.S. system. A pre-application search is available. Trademarks and service marks can be registered for ten-year terms. Registration is constructive notice and prima facie evidence of ownership. There is an anti-dilution statute. Secretary of State, Sacramento, 916-445-9872.

COLORADO

Trademarks and service marks can be registered. Local use is required. A standard form is required for filing (fax: 900-555-1616). There is no dilution statute. The state will search upon written request. There is no intent to use. The term is ten years. There is no presumption of ownership. Secretary of State, Denver, 303-894-2200.

CONNECTICUT

Trademarks and service marks are registrable. The state uses the International Classification system. The state will do searches. The mark must be used in the state. The terms are five years. There is no intent to use. Application and renewal forms must be in a prescribed format. Constructive notice of ownership is available. Secretary of State, Hartford, 860-566-1721 or 860-566-2739.

DISTRICT OF COLUMBIA

Marks are registrable under the Lanham Act.

DELAWARE

Trademarks and service marks are registrable. The terms are ten years. Application and renewal forms are provided. The state will conduct a pre-application search. There is no presumption of ownership. Depart. of State, Dover, 302-736-3073 or 302-739-4111.

FLORIDA

Service marks and trademarks are registrable. There is no intent to use. Use in the state is required for registration. Searches are not available. Official application and renewal forms must be used. The term is ten years. Registration is prima facie evidence of validity and right to use in state. Depart. of State, Tallahassee, 904-487-6000 or 904-488-3680.

GEORGIA
Trademarks and service marks are registrable. Use in the state is required for registration. Prescribed application and renewal forms must be used. Searches by the state may be performed. The term is ten years. There are no presumptions. There is an anti-dilution statute. Secretary of State, Atlanta, 404-656-2861 or 404-656-2861.

HAWAII
Trade names, trademarks and service marks are registrable. Local use is not required. There is an official application form, which is also used for renewals. The initial term is for one year. Renewals have ten-year terms. Searches are not available. There are no presumptions. Depart. of Commerce, Honolulu, 808-586-2727 or 808-586-0255.

IDAHO
Trademarks and service marks are registrable. Searches are available for a fee. Use is required to register. The term is ten years. Official application and renewal forms must be used. There is no intent to use. There are no presumptions. The state has an anti-dilution law. Secretary of State, Boise, 208-334-2300.

ILLINOIS
Trademarks and service marks are registrable. Use in the state is required. A pre-filing search can be performed by the state. The term is ten years. Official application and renewal forms must be used. There are no presumptions. There is an anti-dilution statute. An assignment form can be provided. Secretary of State, Springfield, 217-524-0400 or 217-782-2201.

INDIANA
Trademarks, including service marks, are registrable. Official application forms must be used. There is no intent to use. The state will conduct a preliminary search. There are no presumptions. Secretary of State, Indianapolis, 317-232-6540 or 317-232-6531.

IOWA

Service marks and trademarks are registrable. Local use is required. The term is ten years. There are mandatory application and renewal forms. Free searches are available from the state. There is an anti-dilution law. There are presumptions of validity and right to use throughout the state. Secretary of State, Des Moines, 515-281-5204 or 515-281-2236.

KANSAS

Trademarks and service marks are registrable. Use in the state is required. Application and renewal forms are provided by the state. Searching by the state is free. The term is ten years. There are no presumptions. Secretary of State, Topeka, 913-296-2236.

KENTUCKY

Trademarks and service marks are registrable. Official application and renewal forms must be used. Use in the state is required. The term is five years. An informal telephone search can be performed by the state. There are no presumptions. Secretary of State, Frankfort, 502-564-2848 or 502-564-3490.

LOUISIANA

Trade names, service marks and trademarks are registrable. Local use is required. The term is ten years. Applications and renewal forms are provided by the state. Intent to use is available. There are no presumptions. There is an anti-dilution law. Secretary of State, Baton Rouge, 504-925-4698 or 504-922-1000.

MAINE

Trademarks and service marks are registrable. Local use is required. The term is ten years. There is no intent to use. Prefiling telephone searches can be performed. There are application, renewal and assignment forms. There is a state dilution statute. Depart. of State, Augusta, 207-289-3501 or 207-626-8400.

MARYLAND

Trademarks are registrable. Informal searches are available. Use in the state is required. The term is ten years. There are mandatory application and renewal forms. There are no presumptions. Secretary of State, Annapolis, Maryland, 410-974-5521.

MASSACHUSETTS

Trademarks and service marks are registrable. Use in the state is required. The term is ten years. Applications and renewal forms are provided by the state. There is no pre-application search. There is constructive notice and prima facie right to use. The state has an anti-dilution law. Secretary of State, Boston, 617-727-8329 or 617-727-9180.

MICHIGAN

Trademarks and service marks are registrable. Use in the state is required. The term is ten years. There is no intent to use. Applications and renewal forms are provided by the state. Depart. of Commerce, Lansing, 517-334-6200 or 517-373-2510.

MINNESOTA

Trademarks and service marks are registrable. Local use is required. The term is ten years. A preliminary search can be performed by the state. Application and renewal forms are provided by the state. There is prima facie evidence of right to use and ownership. Secretary of State, St. Paul, 612-296-3266 or 612-296-2079.

MISSISSIPPI

Trademarks and service marks are registrable. Local use is required. The term is ten years. There are official combined application and renewal forms. Searches are not available. There are no presumptions. Secretary of State, Jackson, 601-359-1350.

MISSOURI

Trademarks and service marks are registrable. Local use is required. The term is ten years. Searches are available. Application and renewal forms are provided by the state. There are no presumptions. There is an anti-dilution law. Secretary of State, Jefferson City, 314-751-4756 or 314-751-2379.

MONTANA

Trademarks and service marks are registrable. Application,

renewal and assignment forms are provided. Local use is required. The term is ten years. Searches are available. There are no presumptions. An anti-dilution law is in effect. Secretary of State, Helena, 406-444-3665 or 406-444-3665.

NEBRASKA
Trademarks and service marks are registrable. Local use is required. The term is ten years. Applications, renewals and assignment forms are provided by the state. Searches are available. There are no presumptions. An anti-dilution law is in effect. Secretary of State, Lincoln, 402-471-4079 or 402-471-2554.

NEVADA
Trademarks, trade names and service marks are registrable. The term is five years. Use in the state is required. Searches are available. There are state application and renewal forms. Secretary of State, Carson City. 702-687-5203.

NEW HAMPSHIRE
Trademarks are registrable. Official application and reissue forms must be used. Use in the state is required. The term is ten years. Searches are available. Anti-dilution law is in effect. There are no presumptions. Secretary of State, Concord, 603-271-3244 or 603-271-3242.

NEW JERSEY
Service marks and trademarks are registrable. Forms are not mandatory. Use in the state is required. The term is ten years. There are no presumptions. Secretary of State, Trenton. 609-984-1500.

NEW MEXICO
Trademarks and trade names are registrable. Local use is required. No pre-application search is available. The application and renewal forms are provided by the state. There is no classification system. The term is ten years. There are no presumptions. An anti-dilution law is in effect. Secretary of State, Santa Fe, 505-827-3600.

NEW YORK

Trademarks and service marks are registrable. Local use is required. The term is ten years. Applications and renewal forms are provided by the state. An anti-dilution law is in effect. There are no presumptions. Secretary of State, Albany, 318-474-4770.

NORTH CAROLINA

Trademarks and service marks are registrable. There are official application and renewal forms. Local use is required. The term is ten years. Pre-filing searches are available. There are no presumptions. Secretary of State, Raleigh, 919-733-4161.

NORTH DAKOTA

Trademarks and service marks are registrable. Local use is necessary, but proof is not required. The state will conduct pre-filing searches. There are special application and renewal forms. The term is ten years. There are no presumptions. Secretary of State, Bismarck, 701-224-2992 or 701-224-2900.

OHIO

Trademarks and service marks are registrable. There are prescribed application and renewal forms. The term is ten years. A preliminary search can be performed by the state. There are no presumptions. Secretary of State, Columbus, 614-466-3910 or 614-466-4580.

OKLAHOMA

Trademarks are registrable. The initial term is ten years. Renewal terms are five years. There are no special forms. The state will conduct an informal pre-search. Secretary of State, Oklahoma City, 405-521-3911.

OREGON

Trademarks and service marks are registrable. Application, renewal and assignment forms are available. Pre-application searches can be performed by the state. Use in the state is required. The term is five years. Secretary of State, Salem, 503-378-4381.

PENNSYLVANIA

Trademarks and service marks are registrable. There are no prescribed application or renewal forms. The search is performed at no charge, if the owner calls 717-787-1057. Use in the state is required. The term is ten years. The international classification is used. There are no presumptions. An anti-dilution law is in effect. Secretary of State, Harrisburg, 717-787-1978 or 717-787-7630.

PUERTO RICO[12]

Trademarks and service marks are registrable. Local use is required. Pre-application searches are not available. Application and renewal forms are provided. The term is ten years. Presumption of ownership and right to use are available. Secretary of State, San Juan, 809-722-2121.

RHODE ISLAND

Trademarks and service marks are registrable. Local use is required. The term is ten years. The applications and renewal forms are provided by the state. Presumption of ownership and prima facie right to use are available. An anti-dilution law is in effect. Secretary of State, Providence, 401-277-2521 or 401-277-2357.

SOUTH CAROLINA

Trademarks, trade names and service marks are available. Use in the state is required. The term is five years. There are official forms for applications and renewals. There are no presumptions. An anti-dilution law is in effect. Secretary of State, Columbia, 803-734-2158 or 803-734-2170.

SOUTH DAKOTA

Trademarks and service marks are registrable. There are official application and renewal forms. The term is ten years. The state will do a pre-application search. There is a prima facie right to use. Secretary of State, Pierre, 605-773-3537.

---

[12] U.S. registrations are not recognized unless deposited. Even then, they are subservient to local registrations.

TENNESSEE

Trademarks and service marks are registrable. Use in the state is required. The term is ten years. There are official application and renewal forms. An anti-dilution law is in effect. There are no presumptions. Secretary of State, Nashville, 615-741-0531 or 615-741-2819.

TEXAS

Service marks and trademarks are registrable. Registration is constructive statewide notice. Forms are available but not mandatory. The state will conduct a limited search. Local use is required. The term is ten years. There are special damages for infringement. An anti-dilution law is in effect. Secretary of State, Austin, 512-463-5576 or 512-463-3770.

UTAH

Trademarks and service marks are registrable. The application and renewal forms are the same. Pre-application searches will be performed by the state. Local use is required. The term is ten years. There are no presumptions. Division of Corporations and Commercial Code, Salt Lake City, 801-532-6935 or 801-538-1040.

VERMONT

Trademarks only are registrable. Renewal and application forms are provided by the state. Use in the state is required. The term is ten years. There are no pre-application searches. Registration creates no presumptions. Secretary of State, Montpelier, 802-828-2387 or 802-828-2363.

VIRGINIA

Trademarks and service marks are registrable. Telephone pre-searches will be performed. Application and renewal forms are provided by the state. Local use is required for registration. The old U.S. classification system is used. The term is ten years. State Corporation Commission, Richmond, 804-371-9051 or 786-2441.

WASHINGTON

Trademarks and service marks are registrable. Local use is required. The term is six years. Intent to use is available. Application and renewal forms are provided by the state. An anti-dilution law is in effect. Secretary of State, Olympia, 206-753-7120 or 206-753-7121.

WEST VIRGINIA

Trademarks only are registrable. The term is open. An application form is available, but use is not required. No renewal is necessary. Use in the state is required. Secretary of State, Charleston, 304-342-8000.

WISCONSIN

Trade names, trademarks and service marks are registrable. Application, renewal and assignment forms are provided by the state. Use in the state is not required. The term is ten years. No search is conducted. Intent to use is available. Secretary of State, Madison, 608-266-5653 or 608-266-8888.

WYOMING

All marks are accepted. Applications and renewal forms provided by the state. Use is not required to file. The term is ten years. A search can be requested for a fee. There is no certificate of registration. Office of Secretary of State, Cheyenne, 307-777-7378 or 307-777-7311.

Fifteen

Foreign Trademarks

Trademarks, like patents, are territorial. Rights must be acquired country-by-country, mark-by-mark and class-by-class. Trademark owners who have rights in one country do not have priority elsewhere. This means that someone can see a trademarked product, and unless the trademark is famous, go to Japan, Australia or one of the Common Market countries and register it. Each country becomes a battlefield, where trademark registrations are the spoils. To make matters worse, once products are manufactured in one foreign country, they are frequently exported to other countries.

Common law countries, like the U.S. and Great Britain, have trademark and trade name rights based on use, and even without registration, prior users have enforcement rights against others. In these countries, a trademark owner could forgo registration, if there is actual use, and still be protected. Still, registration is important because of the legal presumptions which accrue.[1]

In civil law countries, trademarks are statutory, rights are granted to the *first to file*, and use is irrelevant to the issue of ownership. Because use is not required to register, this type of system invites pirating, and this has become an accepted entrepreneurial practice in some countries.

Should trademark owners file all of their trademarks in all classes around the world? Even major companies would balk at this. There are 42 classes on the International Classification System.[2] When one multiplies the number of classes of interest by the number of countries, the costs skyrocket. A trademark owner

---

[1] Typical cost is about $1500 per foreign application, per class, per country, assuming that there are not any unusual prosecution difficulties. This does not sound too bad until you factor in the number of classes that may be needed to protect the goods or services.

[2] Expect more at some point, since a revision is under study.

could easily spend $500,000 on a single mark and still only have partial global protection. And if a company has multiple trademarks, or wants to file in color, in logo form or protect a related slogan, the filing costs would escalate proportionately. Then there are renewal and maintenance fees, and to avoid cancellation for non-use, the trademark owner may need to periodically refile to stay ahead in the pecking order.

Nevertheless, foreign trademark protection is essential for companies selling brand name products internationally. Foreign trademarks are costly, but that goes with the territory, and trademark costs usually are in line with other aspects of maintaining an international business.[3] The alternative is being precluded from certain countries, or repurchasing the rights at an even greater cost.

> **FOREIGN TITLE HOLDER**
>
> **So you want to foreign file. What company do you file under? The parent U.S. company, or a foreign subsidiary or distributor? In most cases, you can put title in whichever company you choose, although it never is desirable to put it in a non-owned company. Most companies keep title in the same entity that has it in the U.S. However, some companies have subsidiaries that operate abroad or do the licensing for certain fields, and these companies have title. Another consideration is that some countries, like Taiwan, do not allow sublicensing. In this case, you need to make sure that the title holder is the party licensing the mark. Title can always be changed, but it is costly, and it is important to get it right the first time.**

There is some relief for trademark owners in the form of international trademark conventions and treaties. Well-known (famous) marks, are in theory protectable under Article 6*bis* of

---

[3] The good thing about trademarks is that they usually have ten-year terms with similar renewal terms. If you prorate the costs of obtaining or renewing a trademark over its term, the cost is fairly reasonable.

the Paris Convention. And with modern communications and advertising providing a general awareness of trademarks, enforcement may sometimes be had through state unfair competition laws.[4] U.S. trademark law was also affected by NAFTA and GATT. NAFTA prohibits the use or registration of primarily geographically deceptive misdescriptive terms, unless the mark was in use for ten years before December 8, 1993.[5] Under GATT, which became effective January 1, 1996, abandonment for nonuse is three rather than two years, and the registration of geographically misdescriptive marks for wines and spirits is prohibited.[6]

THE PARIS CONVENTION

The Paris Convention (1883) is the grandfather of international trademark and patent conventions. In various forms, it has been signed by most countries, including the U.S. It is administered by the World Intellectual Property Organization (WIPO). The Paris Convention follows a territorial concept and has three main principles:
(1) Each country promises to give to citizens of other Paris Convention member nations the same protection as it gives its own citizens.
(2) Each member nation promises to provide at least a minimum level of protection.
(3) Priority rights are of the date of first filing if applied for within six months.
No rights are given senior users in other countries. Prior use of a mark in France is not going to give an owner priority rights in the U.S.[7] This means an applicant in one country may

---

[4] For example, in Canada knowledge about trademarks which flows over the border due to travelers and radio and T.V. advertising may be used to establish local use.

[5] North American Free trade Agreement. Effective Dec., 8, 1993.

[6] General Agreement Tariffs and Trade — implementing legislation signed Dec. 8, 1994.

[7] Apparently, use in the U.S. along the border can be used to show use in Canada and establish rights over a subsequent Canadian user.

have senior rights, while that same applicant may be the junior party in another country.[8]

A six-month grace period for filing trademarks in other countries is provided after the owner files in the first country. This may sound useful, but since it limits the trademark owner's coverage to what is registered in the first country, it is not that important. By filing non-convention, coverage can be sought for the *entire* class of goods.[9]

An exception to the territorial rule for trademarks is the "famous trademark doctrine," which holds that famous trademarks should have rights in other countries even without prior local use.[10] The problem is that most trademark owners do not have famous marks, and most owners with famous marks have registered them worldwide anyway. Also, cases have been litigated claiming rights under Article 6 *bis* of the Paris Convention, based on the statutory phrase, "mark or trade names previously used by another in the U.S."[11] How well does this work? Well, it is better than having no recourse, but if the products and marks are not right on, the argument is lost.

An area where the Paris Convention has proved useful is filing counterparts to foreign trademarks in the U.S. under Section 44 of the Lanham Act. The foreign applicant can claim one or more classes of goods by registering or filing in a member country which is the foreigner's country of origin. *The application can be based on a registration in the country of origin, or an application filed in a country of origin within the previous six months.*

Under Section 44, citizens of a country which has treaty rights with the U.S. can file on the same basis as U.S. citizens. Applications may be use-based or filed intent to use. By applying under Section 44, use in the U.S. does not have to be shown to register. However, the free ride the registrant receives is limited, and proof

---

[8] You would think that advertising in the U.S. would count for service mark use but not so. Advertisements don't count unless the services are available locally.

[9] The Paris Convention is useful for patents since the applicant would obtain a priority of one year, and this time is critical since world novelty is usually required.

[10] Thus, Maxim's in Paris enjoined Maxim's in New York.

[11] §2(d)

of use will have to be shown when making a Section 8 declaration.

MADRID AGREEMENTS
(INTERNATIONAL REGISTRATIONS)

The Madrid Arrangement ("Madrid I") was concluded in 1891.[12] The procedures are limited to member countries, thereby precluding the U.S. and other non-signatories.[13] The Madrid Arrangement provides for an international registry where a home country is designated, and then additional countries are listed. When the home registration issues, owners get coverage where they have listed and pay fees accordingly. Countries can be deleted but not added. International trademarks under the Madrid Arrangement have not proved to be that useful because the number of countries participating is limited, and parties from non-member countries are not permitted to file.

The Madrid Protocol

The Madrid Protocol ("Madrid II") was adopted June 27, 1989 and entered into force on December, 1995 after ratification by the U.K., Spain, Sweden and China.[14] The start-up date has been selected as April 1, 1996 to correspond to the Community trademark. The U.S., although a signor, has not acceded.[15]

The Protocol is an improvement over the previous Madrid Arrangement in that an application can be used as the basis for a claim, provided the application subsequently issues as a registration, and a registration is afforded the same protection as if the mark had been registered directly in the country.

---

[12] Under the Protocol in 1971, Belgium, Luxembourg and the Netherlands became a single country for trademark purposes. This is called the BENELUX registration.

[13] Foreign subsidiaries of U.S. companies in the member countries can be title holders of international registrations. However, U.S. corporations operating abroad do not qualify.

[14] Other countries considering or which have joined are Austria, Denmark, Germany, Hungary, Italy, Japan and Portugal.

[15] The reason given is that the EC countries would have one vote under the EC and separate votes as well.

TRADEMARK REGISTRATION TREATY (IRT)

This was signed in 1973 by a group of eight countries, including the U.S. However, this project, which would have created a multi-national filing system, never got off the ground. And with the signing by China to the Madrid Agreements and the U.S. to the Trademark Law Treaty (see below), one can surmise that the IRT, is for all practical purposes, dead.

TRADEMARK LAW TREATY (TLT)

Something new is afoot — the TLT. A set of standard forms and maximum formal requirements are prescribed to harmonize the laws of the countries. The Convention becomes effective three months after five countries have ratified. And now that the U.S. has ratified, it will likely result in some minor changes in U.S. trademark laws and procedures.

THE COMMON MARKET TRADEMARK

The European Community (EC) trademark finally is here after thirty years of discussion and debate.[16] The administrative office is in Alicante, Spain.

> **EC COUNTRIES**
>
> The European Community countries are: Austria, Belgium, the Netherlands, Luxembourg, Denmark, Finland, France, Germany, Greece, Ireland, Italy, Portugal, Spain, Sweden and the United Kingdom. Working languages are Spanish, English, French, German and Italian.

There are many benefits to obtaining Community trademark protection. The Community trademark:

1. requires only a single application;

2. protects against identical marks and similar marks for related goods and services;

---

[16] Effective April 1, 1996.

3. protects well-known marks under the dilution theory;

4. requires use in only one member country to prevent cancellation;

5. applies Paris Convention priority;

6. requires no indication of use;

7. permits multi-class filings;

8. permits joint ownership;

9. can be applied for by non-member countries;

10. covers colors and configurations of goods;

11. is examined on "absolute" and "relative" grounds;

12. is published in all five official languages;

13. allows oppositions by owners of prior trademark rights only;

14. allows the applicant to require an opposer to provide proof of genuine use if the registration is more than five years old;

15. requires opposition costs to be paid by losing party;

16. allows rights to be assignable without goodwill;

17. permits partial assignment of rights to be made;

18. provides claim seniority in individual states based on prior local registrations;

19. allows exclusive or nonexclusive licenses to be granted; and

20. no use is required on renewal.

Marks are examined to determine whether they are capable of acting as trademarks, i.e., they are examined for descriptiveness, etc. A novelty examination is then made, based on prior EC registrations but the results only go to the applicant. It is intended that oppositions will be the primary tool for keeping conflicting marks from being registered.

If the applicant runs into trouble filing the EC application, the applicant can abandon the EC application and convert to national applications. In this way, the applicant keeps the original priority date. This gives the applicant flexibility to test the system on a no-harm basis since it is expected that many EC filings will fail.

DOWNSIDES TO THE EC TRADEMARK

Points to mull over:
1. In obtaining a Community registration, all the trademark owner's rights are put into one basket, which means the owner risks everything during a lawsuit. If the owner loses in one country, he loses everywhere.
2. Registration of retail services is precluded. The author predicts that eventually the world will follow the lead of the U.S. in protecting retail services.
3. No rights are accorded between the application date and registration date. The U.S. has reached a solution to this problem with intent to use applications by having registrations relate back to their filing dates — too bad the Common Market did not follow suit.

It is just a question of time before international trademark owners demand a global trademark system. If governments do not handle the task, in all likelihood, private entities will start to provide the service. A company could be set up as a trademark search and title guarantor ("S&T Co."). If a party wanted to use a mark in a certain territory, the S&T Co. would do a search in the relevant countries and issue the party a title policy with the costs adjusted to reflect the risks.[17] Given the unpredictability, high cost and time delay in obtaining trademarks under current conditions, multi-national companies would jump to participate if a service was able to provide guaranteed trademark rights.

FOREIGN FILING STRATEGY: DARTS ANYONE?

Many well-known marks have already been exposed to the world and are there for the taking. Consequently, trademark owners who wait too long to file internationally find themselves excluded from certain markets or have to buy rights back at a premium from a local party who has registered the marks. On the other hand, if the trademark owner files too early, the regis-

---

[17] This is the same as getting title insurance except you are dealing with intangible property rather than real property.

trations will be subject to attack by third parties for non-use. Timing is critical.

The secret to protecting foreign trademarks is to have a series of cases. The trademark owner needs to originally file with a basic mark in a key class, and then expand the filing program with time so that there are always new applications to support the ones which have matured.

TRADEMARKS IN JAPAN

From a cost and difficulty perspective, Japan tops the list. The filing fees are high and the legal costs are standardized by the government so that you cannot obtain competitive bids. Numerous filings are necessary. Only recently did Japan recognize service marks, but retail services were not included. Then the registrant has the choice of filing in English, Katakana or Chinese Characters. There has to be exact correspondence between the mark which is in use and the registration. For example, usage in color will not support a conventional black on white registration, and usage in stylized letters will not support a trademark with block letters. Also, the scope of protection is limited, since related marks are often approved in the same class. For example, PACIFIC STORES in Int. Class 25 for clothing may be approved over a prior registration for PACIFIC for the same goods.

The procedures for handling trademarks vary considerably from country to country. Each country has special rules and requirements. Japan works differently than Korea, and Korea works differently than China, and China works differently from Thailand, and so forth. The trademark owner should be prepared for surprises and remember that there are no universal rules regarding trademarks.

FOREIGN FILING: OPTIONS

While it is possible for trademark owners to file applications on their own in the U.S., that will not work abroad. Trademark owners should not expect to deal directly with the foreign trademark offices in each country. Most countries require that filings be handled by local attorneys or agents. As a result, the U.S. trademark owner must either use a local trademark attorney in the country of interest or hire a U.S. law firm with foreign contacts. If the trademark owner has selected a few key foreign countries for filing, it is most cost-effective to establish a personal relationship with a foreign firm in each of those countries. In this way, costs can be reduced by direct filing. However, if a trademark owner is embarking on an extensive foreign filing program, it is usually wise to pay a little more and let a foreign trademark specialist in the U.S. handle it. In some cases, the trademark owner can do both: file directly in some of the major markets and hire an attorney to file the rest.

DOCKETING SERVICES

With foreign trademarks, it is *extremely* important to set up some kind of docketing or reminder system so that the owner does not forget about maintenance and renewal fees once the mark is registered. It is vital that the trademark owner keep track of all the dates and deadlines that need to be met. This is especially difficult when marks have been registered in several different countries. Foreign attorneys will normally take responsibility for notifying the owner about fees for the registrations they handled. Intermediary firms will do the same, since processing maintenance fees is an easy way for these firms to make money.

In most countries, payment of the maintenance fees is simple, and trademark owners can usually do it themselves. Trademark docketing programs can be purchased, or an individual computerized docketing system can be prepared using a computer database. However, keeping up with the law changes is difficult, and docketing and maintenance firms are available to do the work.

CROSS REFERENCES

See Appendix One for the International Classification System.

Sixteen

Added Protection Under Lanham Act Section 43(a)

Section 43(a) of the Lanham Act is one of those things that just happened. A fluke of circumstance.[1] No one ever planned for it to become the powerful enforcement tool that it has for false designations of origin and false advertising. Although it is part of the trademark act, it is not based on federal registration. And it can be used in situations where conventional trademark infringement claims would never reach.

Section 43(a) is now recognized as the federal statute to bring actions: (1) for infringement of unregistered trademarks, service marks and trade dress; and (2) for false advertising claims, either by a party concerning his own goods or services, or another's. What makes Section 43(a) so potent is that all the normal trademark infringement remedies are available.[2]

The original version of Section 43(a), which was used from 1947 to 1989, is set forth below:[3]

> Any person who shall affix, apply, or annex, or use, in connection with any goods or services, or any container or containers for goods, a false designation of origin, or any false description or representation, including words

---

[1] Section 43(a) was put in the Lanham Act as a false advertising adjunct to Section 44, which was viewed as the vehicle of the future for developing a general law of unfair competition. The problem was that Section 44 was dependent on the U.S. joining various trademark conventions and treaties, which it never did. So much for Section 44.

[2] §34(a) injunction; §35(a) monetary relief; §36 destruction orders.

[3] For a test of alertness, try reading this late at night. What does it say? The ambiguity of Section 43(a) is what eventually led to its broad enforcement capabilities.

or other symbols tending falsely to describe or represent the same, and shall cause such goods or services to enter into commerce, and any person who shall with knowledge of falsity of such designation of origin or description or representation cause or procure the same to be transported or used in commerce or deliver the same to any carrier to be transported or used, shall be liable to a civil action by any person doing business in the locality falsely indicated as that of origin or the region in which said locality is situated, or by any person who believes that he is or is likely to be damaged by the use of any such false description or representation.

Not having the provision for a general federal law of unfair competition, eventually attorneys and the courts manipulated and stretched Section 43(a) to fit whatever occasions were at hand. When a wrong needed to be remedied, Section 43(a) was called on and then a funny thing happened. Section 43(a) was amended.

FALSE DESIGNATIONS OF ORIGIN

The following are examples of false designation of origin:

- The use of uniforms similar to those of the Dallas Cowboys Cheerleaders in a pornography film (1979).
- The use of a Woody Allen look-alike in advertisements (1988).
- The use of the slogan "Mutant of Omaha" on T-shirts (1987).
- The use of the name "GODIVA" for dog candy (1987).
- The use of "Garbage Pail Kids" which were similar to the "CABBAGE PATCH DOLLS" for cards and stickers (1986).
- The use of the name "GUCCI" for diaper bags (1986).
- The use of "Wench Woman" and "Super Stud" based on the characters of "WONDER WOMAN" and "SUPERMAN" for singing telegrams (1984).

THE 1988 TRADEMARK ACT

The launching pad for Section 43(a) was the 1988 Trademark Act. Section 43(a) was revised to support two thrusts of actions that had developed under the case law — false designations of origin and false advertising. Section 43(a) has become the federal vehicle for the assertion of claims of infringement of *unregistered* trademarks, trade names and trade dress and has been given an enhanced role in false advertising.

Section 43(a) is the only provision in the Lanham Act that allows an action *without having a trademark registration*. Anytime a claim is made for trademark infringement, a cause of action under Section 43(a) can usually be alleged, and often Section 43(a) claims can be made in circumstances where there is no trademark infringement.

PUTTING 43(a) IN PERSPECTIVE

If you are wondering if you can forget registering trademarks and rely on Section 43(a) as your enforcement arm, forget it. Federal registrations, particularly when based on intent to use filings, offer too many advantages to ignore. Section 43(a) is best treated as a supplemental tool or weapon to use when the occasion arises. It should not be viewed a substitute for trademark registrations. If you were going into a gun fight, you would want to take several weapons. Having §43(a) is like carrying a derringer. It is always there, and when you need it, you pull it out. However, given the choice you would preferentially use your magnum. Section 43(a) will get you into federal court, but a replacement for federally registered trademarks, it is not. Registrations in the Principal Register are presumed to be valid, are references as of their filing date, cover the entire U.S. and have the ability to become incontestable.

SECTION 43(a): NEW AND IMPROVED

The revised version of Section 43(a), as it appears in the 1988 Act, is set forth below:

> Any person who in connection with any goods or ser-
> vices, or any container for goods, uses in commerce any
> word, term, name, symbol, or device, or any combina-
> tion thereof, or any false designation of origin, false or
> misleading description of fact, or false or misleading rep-
> resentation of fact, which —
>
> (1) is likely to cause confusion, or to cause mistake, or to
> deceive as to the affiliation of such person with another
> person as to origin, sponsorship, or approval of his or
> her goods services or commercial activities by another
> person, or
> (2) in commercial advertising or promotion, misrepre-
> sents the nature, characteristics, qualities, or geographic
> origin of his or her or another person's goods, services,
> or commercial activities,
>
> shall be liable in a civil action by any person who be-
> lieves that he or she is or is likely to be damaged by such
> act.

The first thing that is evident is that the statute is much easier to read and comprehend than the original version. The two types of causes of action have been separated into subsections. The false designation of origin claim covers uses which are "likely to cause confusion, or to cause mistake, or to deceive as to affili-ation, connection, or association."

This builds into the law the likelihood of confusion test that has always been associated with trademarks. False designation was expanded to cover confusion as to "origin, sponsorship, or approval of goods, services, or commercial activities." The state-ment relating to "commercial activities" is new and appears to reach businesses and other activities. The term "approval of goods and services" meshes with and supports trademark mer-chandising licensing.

The false advertising action was expanded to create a cause of action for trade libel and covers not only false representa-tions about the defendant's goods, services or business, but also false representations about the *plaintiff's* as well. Suit can be brought by any person who believes he is likely to be damaged.

Finally, it was clarified that the normal trademark remedies, including treble damages, profits and attorney fees, apply to Section 43(a) violations.[4]

FALSE DESIGNATION OF ORIGIN

Unregistered Trademarks

Trademarks do not have to be registered. If they are federally registered, the trademark owner may have a cause of action under the Lanham Act. If they are not, the owner has a cause of action under Section 43(a). Since trademarks always relate to particular goods and services, it frequently happens that an owner may have a registration in one area, but the infringement is in another area. Section 43(a) works great in this context. False designation of origin or false advertising which results in a likelihood of confusion is actionable. For example, if "Carrots" and "Cabbages" are used as unregistered trademarks for men's ties with carrot and cabbage designs respectively, and another party uses "Tomatoes" as a mark for ties with tomato designs, a claim of action would lie under Section 43(a) for false designation of origin, since the public would be likely to assume that the same party was behind all three marks.

Trade Names

Trade names can not be directly registered under the Lanham Act. However, we have seen where they can be indirectly registered as trademarks and service marks. Under Section 43(a), an owner can sue for trade name use where it would be a false designation of origin or false advertising. In the above example, if the original party was named "Fresh Vegetable Tie Co." and the copycat was named "Fresh Produce Clothing Company," an action would lie under Section 43(a) for false designation of origin and false advertising relative to the trade names. The similarity of the trade names and the fact that vegetable designs are used by both parties on the ties would carry the action.

---

[4] Damages under Section 43(a) are even easier to recover since the owner is not penalized for not using the "Circle R" symbol.

Trade Dress

A significant case regarding trade dress was handed down by the Supreme Court in 1992. *Two Pesos, Inc. v. Taco Cabana, Inc.* 112 S.Ct. 2753, 23 USPQ2d 1081, 1084 (1992) immediately clothed Section 43(a) in legitimacy. Rarely does the right case come along so quickly, but the perfect trade dress test case presented itself. The *Two Pesos* case concerned the similarity of the interior designs of two restaurants. In the end, the Supreme Court held that the general rules of trademark validity and infringement could be applied under Section 43(a), and that secondary meaning need not be proven where the trade dress is inherently distinctive. *Two Pesos* established that a plaintiff can go into federal court on trade dress alone, which allows actions for packaging designs and configurations which are not normally trademarked.[5] This case was also important because it illustrated that sellers who adopt the same colors and designs as their competitors are at risk. If the copied design is so distinctive that it could have been registered, the competitor can sue, and proof of secondary meaning is not required to win. This gives the Section 43(a) plaintiff a presumption that had previously been reserved to marks registered on the Principal Register.

FALSE ADVERTISING

Section 43(a) was originally intended as a false advertising statute. Under the 1988 Act, it was amended to include non-competitors. Not only does it protect against competitors falsely advertising the quality or attributes of their goods, services and businesses, but it also protects consumers and commercial interests. Trade associations and other non-competitors have brought actions. Any false or misleading description or representation of fact which represents the nature, characteristics, qualities or geographic origin of the advertised goods, services

---

[5] What this does is supplant the common law. You still have common law rights but there are no significant penalties associated with them. Anywhere you have common law rights and places you don't, you have a cause of action under Section 43(a). And with common law you could only go to state court; Section 43(a) will get you into Federal Court.

or commercial activities of the advertiser *or others* is protected. Section 43(a) provides relief against parties that copy the style, format or content of another's advertising, as well as against false descriptions relating to the advertiser's products or services.

FALSE ADVERTISING EXAMPLES

- **Gelatin snacks were enjoined because the product had no gelatin (1993).**
- **An advertising claim that a rainsuit was waterproof was false since it was only partially waterproof (1992).**
- **A defendant's insertion of a copyright notice in place of the plaintiff's was ruled an actionable wrong (1989).**
- **An improper use of the Underwriters logo was deemed false advertising (1983).**
- **A claim that a product was "as advertised on TV" was deemed false where there had been no advertising (1972).**
- **The resale of trademarked second goods as originals was false advertising (1992).**

To have standing to bring an action, the plaintiff need only show belief that he or she would likely be damaged as a result of the advertising. Damage is presumed in the case of comparative advertising, although the misrepresentation must be material rather than trivial. There is no need to prove actual deception. Anything claimed in an advertisement about a product or service, *or a competitor's product or service,* that is incorrect or misleading is actionable.

REMEDIES

Pre-1989, damages under Section 43(a) were limited, and there was reluctance to accord Section 43(a) the same remedies as for infringements of marks, or to allow attorney fees. The 1988 Act held that the trademark infringement remedies listed in Sections 34, 35 and 36 apply for Section 43(a) violations the same as any other infringement.

STANDING TO SUE

Not everyone can sue, only those that have standing. Due to the wording of Section 43(a), only parties who "believe that they are likely to be damaged" have standing to sue. That means that owners of rights can sue, but so can non-owners, such as exclusive licensees or distributors. In order to show standing, parties bringing suit must show a special relationship and show that they are likely to be damaged.

JURISDICTION

Under Section 43(a), federal jurisdiction attaches if the goods, services or businesses are performed in interstate commerce, or in the case of false advertising claims, if the advertising occurs in interstate commerce. As expected, the 1988 amendment has been seized upon to cover an expanded melange of fact situations.

CROSS REFERENCES

See Chapter Seventeen on infringements. The Addendum to this chapter presents an assortment of recent Section 43(a) cases.

ADDENDUM ONE: POST-1988 SECTION 43(A) CASES

- "Hard Rain Cafe" for heat transfers on clothing was found to infringe "HARD ROCK CAFE" for restaurant services and merchandising items.
- False endorsement claims arising out of the unauthorized imitation of a singer's voice were actionable.
- A toy robot dressed in a wig, gown and jewelry which was posed next to a "WHEEL OF FORTUNE" game board raised an issue of fact as to likelihood of confusion.
- The resale of second goods without a notice to the purchaser to that effect was found to be a violation of Section 43(a).
- "Michelob Oily" in a magazine parody was found to be confusing as to sponsorship.
- The unauthorized use of the "Spuds McKenzie" image on T-shirts was ruled actionable.
- A defendant was enjoined from using a picture of a plaintiff's wallet in advertising.

Seventeen

Litigation

It seems to be the nature of trademarks, since they are always before the public, that other parties either infringe them or do not respect them. And the more valuable a trademark, the more likely it is that there will be infringers. Trademark owners are charged with policing the marketplace for infringers and when cease and desist letters are ignored, they are forced to bring the matter before the courts.

Most trademark owners are hesitant to initiate a lawsuit, since suits are traditionally expensive, and there is no guarantee for recovery. Initiating a law suit is also very time-consuming. On the other hand, the trademark owner cannot sit idly by and do nothing, since that will result in the trademark being weakened. This is why there is, and probably always will be, heavy trademark litigation. If a trademark owner knows of multiple infringers, it is generally accepted that the owner is only obligated to pursue one at a time. The owner will usually pick the easiest target, the party causing the most harm or someone with whom he or she has an ax to grind.

When considering whether or not to bring a law suit, it is important to remember that communications between a plaintiff and the plaintiff's attorney are privileged, which means that they are not subject to discovery, assuming that the privilege is not waived. In addition, confidential business information and trade secrets can be protected by secrecy orders.

However, no suit should be entered into lightly, since there may be counterclaims. Consequently, any previous dealings the trademark owner has had with the infringing party, or concerning the infringed property, should be carefully reviewed. Also, the trademark owner will want to reinvestigate the infringing party to determine the circumstances of use. It may turn out that the infringer has an earlier first usage date than the trademark owner.

Another matter that trademark owners need be concerned about is the existence of third party rights. Trademark rights are always relative. If a third party has superior rights over the two parties involved in a trademark infringement suit, that makes no difference. So long as the first party has rights superior to the second party, the first party will prevail, even though an unrelated third party may have rights superior to both. However, if the second party acquires the third party's rights, the first party may suddenly be on the losing end of the litigation.[1]

Still another consideration is the location of the infringer. The trademark owner may discover an infringer, but if he is in a remote market territory, the trademark owner may not be able to bring suit for an injunction. In *Dawn Donut Co. v. Hart's Food Stores, Inc.*, 267 F.2d 358, 362 (2d Cir. 1959), the court ruled that the registrant is only able to exercise his rights against a junior user *at the time he is likely to enter the junior user's market territory.*[2]

Consider the following example. Fred operates a donut shop in Dallas, Texas under the mark "Blue Skies," and Jerry opens up a donut shop in Los Angeles, California, under the name "Blue Sky Donuts." Even though Fred obtains a federal registration on the Principal Register for "Blue Skies" as a service mark for restaurant services which pre-dates Jerry's use, Fred is precluded from bringing suit to enjoin Jerry, until Fred can show a likelihood of confusion. If Fred franchises in California, then the test is met, and an injunction can be obtained.

CAUSES OF ACTION

The plaintiff in a trademark litigation suit usually has a choice of causes of actions and forums. Grounds for action include: (1) federal trademark infringement under Section 32 of the Lanham Act; (2) violation of Section 43(a) of the Lanham Act; (3) common law trademark infringement; (4) state trademark infringement; (5) violation of federal or state anti-dilution laws; (6) federal and state actions arising from trademark coun-

---

[1] The trademark area is one of the few areas of the law where you can play legal hopscotch since rights of other parties can be tacked on to yours.

[2] Apparently, the reasoning is that only then can there be likelihood of confusion.

terfeiting; and (7) violation of state fair business practices or consumer protection statutes.

Federal Trademark Infringement

Section 32 of the Lanham Act reads as follows:

(1) any person who shall, without the consent of the registrant —
(a) use in commerce any reproduction, counterfeit, copy, or colorable imitation of a registered mark in connection with the sale, offering for sale, distribution, or advertising of any goods or services on or in connection with which such use is likely to cause mistake, or to deceive; or
(b) reproduce, counterfeit, copy or colorably imitate a registered mark and apply such reproduction, counterfeit, copy or colorable imitation to labels, signs, prints, packages, wrappers, receptacles, or advertisements intended to be used in commerce upon or in connection with the sale of, offering for sale, distribution, or advertising of goods or services on or in connection with which such use is likely to cause confusion, or to cause mistake, or to deceive,
shall be liable in a civil action by the registrant for the remedies hereinafter provided.[3]

ACTIONS AGAINST STATE GOVERNMENTS

States represent some of the deepest pockets around and are no longer immune from being sued for trademark infringement. State immunity ended in 1992 with the enactment of The Trademark Remedy Clarification Act. Now claims can be brought against state governments based on infringements that occurred after October 27, 1992.

---

[3] Under §32(b), recovery of profits and damages cannot be obtained unless the acts were committed with the knowledge that they were likely to cause confusion, mistake or to deceive.

Likelihood of confusion is the test for trademark infringement. This means that the plaintiff must prove that there is a likelihood that an appreciable number of ordinary consumers will be confused by the defendant's actions.[4] Tests for determining likelihood of confusion include:

- **Similarity of the marks.** The court will look at the appearance of the marks and consider how they are pronounced and their meanings. The marks as a whole should be compared without dissection.
- **Closeness of the goods or services.** The test is whether the average purchaser would believe they both derived from the same source.
- **The trademark's strength.** It is descriptive? Arbitrary marks are entitled to strong protection, while descriptive marks are limited in scope.
- **Advertising and sales.** The more a mark is advertised, the more likely the public will be confused by other users.
- **The relative length of use by the parties.** The longer a party has used the mark, the stronger his or her rights will be relative to a newcomer.
- **The sophistication of the purchasers.** Industrial users are not as likely to be confused as individuals.
- **The extent of use by third parties.** If a mark is used by numerous third parties, it will be considered weak.
- **The number and types of instances of actual confusion.**
- **The relative quality of the parties' goods and services.**
- **The intent of the defendant.** Was there good faith or was the defendant trying to play on the plaintiff's goodwill?

These tests demonstrate a common sense approach. Depending on the circumstances, some factors are given more weight than others. The same tests are applicable to common law infringements and to establishing likelihood of confusion under Section 43(a) and state statutes.

---

[4] Examples of actual confusion are usually hard to come by. The best readily available proof often comes from survey evidence.

Violation of Section 43(a)

There are two basic types of actions. Actions for infringement of unregistered trademarks and trade dress, and actions for false advertising. (See Chapter Sixteen.) These can be plead in the alternative with claims for infringement under Section 32.

Common Law Trademark Infringement

Anyone who is in business and using a trade name or trademark has common law rights. Common laws rights still exist even though an owner has state or federal registrations. And if an owner loses its registrations, the common law rights often continue unabated. They can be asserted in state court or in federal court in connection with federal claims.

State Trademark Infringement

For this to apply, the owner has to have a trademark registration for the marks in the state. A claim can be filed in state court or combined with federal counts in federal court. Most state trademarks equate with the rights under common law.

Violation of Anti-dilution Laws

Until recently, there was no federal dilution law, and if a trademark owner wanted to claim dilution, he had to rely on various state anti-dilution statutes. In January of 1996, legislation was signed providing for a federal cause of action for dilution of famous marks.[5]

Trademark Counterfeiting

Most states had adopted counterfeiting statutes of their own before the federal government did it in 1984. Federal legislation

---

[5] The Federal Dilution Act of 1996. This adds Section 43(c)(1) to the Lanham Act, which entitles owners of famous marks to injunctive relied against unauthorized commercial use which dilutes the distinctive quality of the plaintiff's marks.

does not preempt state counterfeiting laws, so that state and federal remedies continue to coexist. The federal anti-counterfeiting laws have both civil and criminal sanctions.

State Fair Business and Consumer Protection Laws

Fair business and consumer protection laws are state-based unfair competition laws which were codified before Section 43(a) became a force. Plaintiffs can couple state claims with a federal action.

REMEDIES

Multiple remedies for trademark infringement are available. Injunctive relief, damages, recovery of profits, seizure and destruction of the infringing property, attorney fees and court costs can be obtained.

Injunctions

An injunction is the traditional relief for trademark infringement. The plaintiff gets a court order for the defendant to stop the action that had been complained about. There are several forms of injunctions: temporary restraining orders, preliminary injunctions and permanent injunctions.

> **FORMS OF INJUNCTIVE RELIEF**
>
> Injunctive relief can take many forms. The plaintiff can get an injunction against continued use by the defendant. The plaintiff can have infringing items recalled. The plaintiff can get the defendant to change his trade name or trademark. The plaintiff can have the court require the defendant to use a disclaimer of association. The plaintiff can have the defendant issue corrective advertising and take other actions appropriate under the circumstances.

A preliminary injunction is viewed as an extraordinary remedy where the plaintiff wants the defendant to stop use immediately. The courts will consider the following when deciding whether to issue a preliminary injunction:

- whether the plaintiff is likely to succeed on the merits of the case;
- whether the plaintiff can show irreparable injury if the action continues;
- whether an injunction will maintain the status quo;
- whether the hardships balance the plaintiff; and
- whether the injunction will protect third parties.

If an injunction is granted and the defendant fails to comply, the plaintiff can ask the judge for a contempt of court order. In this situation, the defendant can be put in jail or fined in order to get compliance.

Monetary Damages

Monetary damages are available under Section 35 of the Lanham Act for infringement suits brought under Sections 32 and 43(a). Section 35 gives the court discretion to award treble damages, profits increased by an amount deemed to be just and attorney fees.

To obtain monetary awards, damages of some degree have to be shown. One common measure is what a reasonable royalty would have been. If corrective advertising had to be undertaken by the plaintiff, the advertising costs could be claimed. If the plaintiff lost business, the profits associated with the loss of business can be asserted.

Treble damages amount to triple the actual damages shown by the plaintiff. Treble damages are intended as compensation and not as a penalty. In order for the plaintiff to be awarded treble damages, the plaintiff will have to establish the defendant's willfulness of infringement and non-cooperation.

Punitive damages are precluded under the Lanham Act, but may be available under some state statutes. (This is one reason for asserting state claims.)

Recovery of Profits

Recovery of the defendant's profits are usually limited to instances of intentional infringement. The plaintiff need only show gross sales. The defendant is required to prove any deductions. A recovery of enhanced profits can be awarded.

Attorney Fees

Reasonable attorney fees may be awarded to the prevailing party in exceptional circumstances. Sometimes the attorney fees will outweigh the profits or proven damages. But parties to a suit should not expect to recover total attorney fees, since the system does not work that way. Reasonable fees are always viewed by a court as being less than they are. Plaintiffs are most likely to recover attorney fees for willful infringements, or where the defendant's activities were fraudulent, e.g., where the defendant used the mark after being denied permission by the plaintiff.

The plaintiff can be ordered to pay attorney fees as well, e.g., where the plaintiff brought suit in bad faith without making a reasonable investigation, or where the plaintiff's claims had no substance.

Court Costs

Court costs are available to the prevailing party as a matter of course. These costs are usually insignificant.

Other Actions

Among other remedies, a federal judge can cancel the defendant's trademark registrations, prohibit the importation of infringing goods and order the destruction or other disposition of infringing goods.

CROSS REFERENCES

See Chapter Sixteen on Section 43(a) causes of action.

Eighteen

Marketing Trademarks

The trademark owner has several choices in marketing a trademark. This chapter explores the alternatives. The owner can market a product or provide a service using the trademark. The owner can license manufacturers or users. The owner can sell or assign the trademark rights, or the owner can form a joint venture. The best alternative depends on the trademark, the goods or services, the competition, the marketplace and the owner's capabilities.

Once the trademark owner receives a trademark registration or vested rights in a mark through intent to use, the rights will expire if not used. If the trademark has been registered, the registrant will have to provide proof of use during the sixth year, and renew every ten years or else the registration will lapse. Rights could lapse even sooner as a result of non-use, since a registration is presumed to be abandoned if there has been no use of the mark for more than three years.

For intent to use applications, the applicant will have six months from the notice of allowance to provide a statement of use. If the applicant is willing to spend another $100 per class, a six-month extension can be obtained, so that in essence, the intent to use applicant has a year before the rights toll.[1] In addition, the intent to use applicant must be concerned about *the scope of the goods and services* covered in the intent to use application. When filing the statement of use, the applicant will have to restrict the goods and services to those actually in use. This means the applicant needs to bring out all the products or services concurrently, and do so quickly, rather than piecemeal them.

---

[1] Beyond this, the applicant can ask for up to two additional six month extensions but the applicant must show good cause. In any case, the term can not extend beyond 36 months of the application date.

Finally, use must be *legitimate commercial use in ordinary trade*. Token use is no longer considered sufficient to issue or maintain a registration.

MARKETING BY THE TRADEMARK OWNER

If the trademark owner has an established business and is using the new trademark simply to expand the product line or rename a product, exploiting the mark is relatively easy, since there is already a market. The trademark owner can concentrate on preparing the final product design and work on advertising and graphics. The owner can even do comparative test marketing and conduct surveys. Under these circumstances, the trademark owner can usually "go it alone" and market the new product without the use of a new business partner. In this scenario, there is little purpose in licensing, although a joint venture could be profitable and should remain a possibility where other parties are able to make a significant contribution.

MARKETING BY LICENSING

On the other hand, building a business from scratch is hard work. The owner's time is consumed by day-to-day business concerns which include how to get the product manufactured and how market it. Trademark owners who are unwilling or unable to take the financial risks associated with starting a business often turn to licensing. By granting a trademark license to a manufacturer who is already in business, the trademark owner is able to generate profits in the form of royalties from the manufacturer's sales, without risking a great deal of capital. In these situations, the trademark owner acts as the licensor — the party granting the rights. The manufacturer is the licensee — the party who is granted rights to use the trademark on a product or in connection with a service.

The Lanham Act treats use by licensees the same as use by the trademark owner. At one time, it was considered that the owner had to use a mark *personally* before licensing it; however, this contention has been abandoned. Now, use by a licensee inures directly to the benefit of the trademark owner, and this can serve as a basis to issue the registration in the licensor's name.

Trademark licensors are required to exercise quality control over their licensees, and if they fail, their registrations are open to attack. Therefore, licensors should not assume their work is done once the license agreement has been signed. Directly or indirectly, the licensor remains responsible for the quality of the goods and services.

What kind of license can the licensor grant? Licenses can be exclusive or non-exclusive. Some licensors are better off licensing non-exclusively, which means several companies will have the rights to exploit the trademark. This concept works well when the licensor has a hot trademark, and everyone wants to get on the bandwagon. In the case of a trademark which is not in demand, it is often difficult to get licensees. In order to interest a manufacturer, the licensor may have to grant the manufacturer an exclusive right to use the trademark.[2]

LICENSING AGENTS

As in every other occupation, there are good licensing agents and there are bad licensing agents. Some are substantial companies, and some are one-person operations. Some will only represent major companies, and some will take on promising projects whatever their source.[3]

Presumably, a licensor will hire a licensing agent because that agent has contacts with manufacturers. When seeking to hire an agent, it is advisable for the licensor to investigate the agent's track record and determine what marks he or she has licensed. The licensor should ask to see the agent's standard form agreement. There may be a wide variance of terms from agent to agent.

---

[2] Exclusive licenses do not have to be forever and all-inclusive. The licensor can put a time limit on them or limit them to a particular field or product category. Also, the licensor should have performance standards built in the license agreement which the licensee has to meet to keep exclusivity.

[3] Licensing agents should cover their own expenses and receive a percentage of the royalties for their services. Purported agents that charge fees may be in the business of representing licensors rather than licensing trademarks.

Licensing agents will typically receive twenty to thirty-five percent of the royalties. Some agents want to grant sublicenses; others will allow the licensor to execute the agreements with third parties. From a trademark perspective, dealing directly with the sublicensee is better, since quality control is stronger. An exclusive licensing agent representation agreement with an initial term of two to five years is typical.[4]

NOT INVENTED HERE SYNDROME

Even if you have a great idea and have obtained the proper trademark protection for it, you may find it difficult to convince another company to market it. Many companies are used to generating their own ideas. Also, they are biased against receiving ideas from outsiders because this could place them under confidentiality obligations.

ASSIGNMENT OF TRADEMARK RIGHTS

An intent to use application cannot be assigned by the applicant (unless it is part of the entire assets of the applicant's business to which the mark pertains) until proof of use has been submitted to and accepted by the Patent and Trademark Office. However, there are ways around this. If the applicant locates a purchaser but has not made use of the trademark, the applicant can enter into an exclusive license and then agree to assign the mark at a future time.[5]

JOINT VENTURES

A joint venture is an association between two or more parties for a particular business purpose. Usually the parties have an operating agreement defining their respective duties and

---

[4] A list of licensing agents is available from the Licensing Industry Merchandising Association (LIMA); 212-768-9887.

[5] Proceeds from the assignment should qualify as capital gains, if that has any significance.

rights.[6] A trademark owner should consider a joint venture involving trademark rights where the other party has something to bring to the table. The party, for example, could be a manufacturer or a financier. Joint ventures in foreign countries in connection with trademark licensing or franchising are very common.

THINGS TO COME

Trademarks will likely become even more of an important marketing tool in the future. With impending global communication PC-to-PC, trademark licensors will be hunted down relentlessly. New licensing procedures will be developed to meet the new practicalities of doing business. The not-too-distant future will likely see the posting of available licenses, terms and conditions on computer bulletin boards, and they will be accepted by e-mail.

ASSOCIATIONS

The following associations should be considered for membership or as sources of materials.

- The International Trademark Association (INTA) is a worldwide association of trademark attorneys, companies and parties interested in trademarks. INTA publishes a number of books about trademarks, including **The U.S. Trademark Law: Rules of Practice, Forms and Federal Statutes**. For information call 212-768-9887 or fax 212-768-7796. INTA's address is 1133 Avenue of the Americas, New York, NY 10036-6710. It has a Web site at http://www.inta.org.
- The Licensing Executives Society (LES) is an international association of companies and individuals interested in licensing intellectual property rights (trademarks, copyrights, patents, and trade secrets). Its newsletter, *Les*

---

[6] There generally are no state joint venture laws which define provisions where the parties haven't agreed on the terms like there are for partnerships.

Nouvelles, is useful and informative for those involved in foreign activities. For information, call 216-241-3940. LES's home page is http://www.les.com, or write Suite 403, 1444 West 10th Street, Cleveland, Ohio 44117.
* The Licensing and Merchandising Association (LIMA) is largely an association of entertainment and character licensors and licensees. For information call 212-244-1944.

All of the above associations have annual meetings, although INTA and LES have become so large that you get lost in the shuffle. The least expensive organization to join is LES. If you are interested in sourcing trademark attorneys, obtain a copy of INTA's membership directory. The LES Membership directory is also useful for finding contacts at companies and in different cities and countries.

GOVERNMENT MATERIALS

The following materials are available from the government:
* A free booklet entitled "Basic Facts About Trademarks" can be ordered by calling 703-557-INFO or by writing: U.S. Department of Commerce, Patent and Trademark Office, Washington, DC 20231. This book is also available for a nominal fee from the Government Printing Office.
* The U.S. Patent and Trademark Office has a web site at www@uspto.gov. Various trademark-related materials can be printed out and downloaded, including a roster of patent attorneys. A current fee schedule for various Patent and Trademark Office charges is also available.
* Copies of trademark registrations can be ordered from Patent and Trademark customer service at 703-305-4350. The fax line is 703-305-8759. Copies are $3.00 each.

CROSS REFERENCES

The Glossary provides a review of trademark terms and concepts.

Appendix One

International Schedule of Classes of Goods and Services

GOODS

1   Chemicals used in industry, science and photography, as well as in agriculture, horticulture and forestry; unprocessed artificial resins, unprocessed plastics; manures; fire extinguishing compositions; tempering and soldering preparations; chemical substances for preserving foodstuffs; tanning substances; adhesives used in industry.

2   Paints, varnishes, lacquers; preservatives against rust and against deterioration of wood; colorants; mordants; raw natural resins; metals in foil and powder form for painters, decorators, printers and artists.

3   Bleaching preparations and other substances for laundry use; cleaning, polishing, scouring and abrasive preparations; soaps; perfumery, essential oils, cosmetics, hair lotions; dentifrices.

4   Industrial oils and greases; lubricants; dust absorbing, wetting and binding compositions; fuels (including motor spirit) and illuminants; candles, wicks.

5   Pharmaceutical, veterinary and sanitary preparations; dietetic substances adapted for medical use, food for babies; plasters, materials for dressings; material for stopping teeth, dental wax; disinfectants; preparations for destroying vermin; fungicides, herbicides.

6   Common metals and their alloys; metal building materials; transportable buildings of metal; materials of metal for railway tracks; non-electric cables and wires of common metal; ironmongery, small items of metal

hardware; pipes and tubes of metal; safes; goods of common metal not included in other classes; ores.

7   Machines and machine tools; motors and engines (except for land vehicles); machine coupling and transmission components (except for land vehicles); agricultural implements; incubators for eggs.

8   Hand tools and implements (hand operated); cutlery; side arms; razors.

9   Scientific, nautical, surveying, electric, photographic, cinematographic, optical, weighing, measuring, signaling, checking (supervision), life-saving and teaching apparatus and instruments; apparatus for recording, transmission or reproduction of sound or images; magnetic data carriers, recording discs; automatic vending machines and mechanisms for coin operated apparatus; cash registers, calculating machines, data processing equipment and computers; fire-extinguishing apparatus.

10   Surgical, medical, dental and veterinary apparatus and instruments, artificial limbs, eyes and teeth; orthopedic articles; suture materials.

11   Apparatus for lighting, heating, steam generating, cooking, refrigerating, drying, ventilating, water supply and sanitary purposes.

12   Vehicles; apparatus for locomotion by land, air or water.

13   Firearms; ammunition and projectiles; explosives; fireworks.

14   Precious metals and their alloys and goods in precious metals or coated therewith, not included in other classes; jewelry, precious stones; horological and chronometric instruments.

15   Musical instruments.

16   Paper, cardboard and goods made from these materials, not included in other classes; printed matter; bookbinding material; photographs; stationery; adhesives for stationery or household purposes; artists' materials; paint brushes; typewriters and office requisites (except furniture); instructional and teaching material (except apparatus); playing cards; printers' type; printing blocks.

17   Rubber, gutta-percha, gum asbestos, mica and goods made from these materials and not included in other classes; plastics in extruded form for use in manufacture; packing, stopping and insulating materials; flexible pipes, not of metal.

18   Leather and imitations of leather, and goods made of these materials and not included in other classes; animal skins, hides; trunks and traveling bags; umbrellas, parasols and walking sticks; whips, harness and saddlery.

19   Building materials (non-metallic); non-metallic rigid pipes for building asphalt, pitch and bitumen; non-metallic transportable buildings; monuments, not of metal.

20   Furniture, mirrors, picture frames; goods (not included in other classes) of wood, cork, reed, cane, wicker, horn, bone, ivory, whalebone, shell, amber, mother-of-pearl, meerschaum and substitutes for all these materials, or of plastics.

21   Household or kitchen utensils and containers (not of precious metal or coated therewith); combs and sponges; brushes (except paint brushes); brush-making materials; articles for cleaning purposes; steel wool; unworked or semi-worked glass (except glass used in

building); glassware, porcelain and earthenware not included in other classes.

22 Ropes, string, nets, tents, awnings, tarpaulins, sails, sacks and bags (not included in other classes); padding and stuffing materials (except of rubber or plastics); raw fibrous textile materials.

23 Yarns and threads, for textile use.

24 Textiles and textile goods, not included in other classes; bed and table covers.

25 Clothing, footwear, headgear.

26 Lace and embroidery, ribbons and braid; buttons, hooks and eyes, pins and needles; artificial flowers.

27 Carpets, rugs, mats and matting, linoleum and other materials for covering existing floors; wall hangings (non-textile).

28 Games and playthings; gymnastic and sporting articles not included in other classes; decorations for Christmas trees.

29 Meat, fish, poultry and game; meat extracts; preserved, dried and cooked fruits and vegetables; jellies, jams, fruit sauces; eggs, milk and milk products; edible oils and fats.

30 Coffee, tea, cocoa, sugar, rice, tapioca, sago, artificial coffee; flour and preparations made from cereals, bread, pastry and confectionery, honey, treacle; yeast, baking-powder, salt, mustard; vinegar, sauces (condiments); spices; ice.

31 Agricultural, horticultural and forestry products and grains not included in other classes; live animals; fresh

fruits and vegetables; seeds, natural plants and flowers; foodstuffs for animals, malt.

32　Beers; mineral and aerated waters and other non-alcoholic drinks; fruit drinks and fruit juices; syrups and other preparations for making beverages.

33　Alcoholic beverages (except beers).

34　Tobacco; smokers' articles; matches.

SERVICES

35　Advertising; business management; business administration; office functions.

36　Insurance; financial affairs; monetary affairs; real estate affairs.

37　Building construction; repair; installation services.

38　Telecommunications.

39　Transport; packaging and storage of goods; travel arrangement.

40　Treatment of materials.

41　Education; providing of training; entertainment; sporting and cultural activities.

42　Providing of food and drink; temporary accommodation; medical, hygienic and beauty care; veterinary and agricultural services; legal services; scientific and industrial research; computer programming; services that cannot be placed in other classes.

Appendix Two

Sample Trademark/Service Mark Application, Principal Register, With Declaration

TRADEMARK/SERVICE MARK APPLICATION, PRINCIPAL REGISTER, WITH DECLARATION	MARK (Word(s) and/or Design)	CLASS NO. (If known)

TO THE ASSISTANT SECRETARY AND COMMISSIONER OF PATENTS AND TRADEMARKS:

APPLICANT'S NAME:

APPLICANT'S BUSINESS ADDRESS:
(Display address exactly as
it should appear on registration)

APPLICANT'S ENTITY TYPE: (Check one and supply requested information)

	Individual - Citizen of (Country):
	Partnership - State where organized (Country, if appropriate): _____ Names and Citizenship (Country) of General Partners: _____
	Corporation - State (Country, if appropriate) of Incorporation:
	Other (Specify Nature of Entity and Domicile):

GOODS AND/OR SERVICES:

Applicant requests registration of the trademark/service mark shown in the accompanying drawing in the United States Patent and Trademark Office on the Principal Register established by the Act of July 5, 1946 (15 U.S.C. 1051 et. seq., as amended) for the following goods/services (SPECIFIC GOODS AND/OR SERVICES MUST BE INSERTED HERE):

BASIS FOR APPLICATION: (Check boxes which apply, but never both the first AND second boxes, and supply requested information related to each box checked.)

[ ] Applicant is using the mark in commerce on or in connection with the above identified goods/services. (15 U.S.C. 1051(a), as amended.) Three specimens showing the mark as used in commerce are submitted with this application.
• Date of first use of the mark in commerce which the U.S. Congress may regulate (for example, interstate or between the U.S. and a foreign country):
• Specify the type of commerce: _____
(for example, interstate or between the U.S. and a specified foreign country)
• Date of first use anywhere (the same as or before use in commerce date): _____
• Specify manner or mode of use of mark on or in connection with the goods/services: _____

(for example, trademark is applied to labels, service mark is used in advertisements)

[ ] Applicant has a bona fide intention to use the mark in commerce on or in connection with the above identified goods/services. (15 U.S.C. 1051(b), as amended.)
• Specify intended manner or mode of use of mark on or in connection with the goods/services: _____

(for example, trademark will be applied to labels, service mark will be used in advertisements)

[ ] Applicant has a bona fide intention to use the mark in commerce on or in connection with the above identified goods/services, and asserts a claim of priority based upon a foreign application in accordance with 15 U.S.C. 1126(d), as amended.
• Country of foreign filing: _____ • Date of foreign filing: _____

[ ] Applicant has a bona fide intention to use the mark in commerce on or in connection with the above identified goods/services and, accompanying this application, submits a certification or certified copy of a foreign registration in accordance with 15 U.S.C. 1126(e), as amended.
Country of registration: _____ • Registration number: _____

NOTE: Declaration, on Reverse Side, MUST be Signed

PTO Form 1478 (REV. 8/92)   U.S DEPARTMENT OF COMMERCE/Patent and Trademark Office
OMB No. 0651-0009 (Exp. 6/30/95)

DECLARATION

The undersigned being hereby warned that willful false statements and the like so made are punishable by fine or imprisonment, or both, under 18 U.S.C. 1001, and that such willful false statements may jeopardize the validity of the application or any resulting registration, declares that he/she is properly authorized to execute this application on behalf of the applicant; he/she believes the applicant to be the owner of the trademark/service mark sought to be registered, or, if the application is being filed under 15 U.S.C. 1051(b), he/she believes applicant to be entitled to use such mark in commerce; to the best of his/her knowledge and belief no other person, firm, corporation, or association has the right to use the above identified mark in commerce, either in the identical form thereof or in such near resemblance thereto as to be likely, when used on or in connection with the goods/services of such other person, to cause confusion, or to cause mistake, or to deceive; and that all statements made of his/her own knowledge are true and that all statements made on information and belief are believed to be true.

DATE   SIGNATURE

TELEPHONE NUMBER   PRINT OR TYPE NAME AND POSITION

INSTRUCTIONS AND INFORMATION FOR APPLICANT

TO RECEIVE A FILING DATE, THE APPLICATION MUST BE COMPLETED AND SIGNED BY THE APPLICANT AND SUBMITTED ALONG WITH:

1. The prescribed FEE ($210.00) for each class of goods/services listed in the application;
2. A DRAWING PAGE displaying the mark in conformance with 37 CFR 2.52;
3. If the application is based on use of the mark in commerce, THREE (3) SPECIMENS (evidence) of the mark as used in commerce for each class of goods/services listed in the application. All three specimens may be in the nature of: (a) labels showing the mark which are placed on the goods; (b) photographs of the mark as it appears on the goods, (c) brochures or advertisements showing the mark as used in connection with the services.
4. An APPLICATION WITH DECLARATION (this form) - The application must be signed in order for the application to receive a filing date. Only the following person may sign the declaration, depending on the applicant's legal entity: (a) the individual applicant; (b) an officer of the corporate applicant; (c) one general partner of a partnership applicant; (d) all joint applicants.

SEND APPLICATION FORM, DRAWING PAGE, FEE, AND SPECIMENS (IF APPROPRIATE) TO:

U.S. DEPARTMENT OF COMMERCE
Patent and Trademark Office, Box TRADEMARK
Washington, D.C. 20231

Additional information concerning the requirements for filing an application is available in a booklet entitled Basic Facts About Trademarks, which may be obtained by writing to the above address or by calling: (703) 308-HELP.

This form is estimated to take an average of 1 hour to complete, including time required for reading and understanding instructions, gathering necessary information, recordkeeping, and actually providing the information. Any comments on this form, including the amount of time required to complete this form, should be sent to the Office of Management and Organization, U.S. Patent and Trademark Office, U.S. Department of Commerce, Washington, D.C. 20231, and to Paperwork Reduction Project 0651-0009, Office of Information and Regulatory Affairs, Office of Management and Budget, Washington, D.C. 20503. Do NOT send completed forms to either of these addresses.

Appendix Three

Sample Certification Mark Application, Principal Register, With Declaration

CERTIFICATION MARK APPLICATION, PRINCIPAL REGISTER, WITH DECLARATION	MARK (Word(s) and/or Design)
	CLASS [ ] A. Goods [ ] B. Services

TO THE ASSISTANT SECRETARY AND COMMISSIONER OF PATENTS AND TRADEMARKS:

APPLICANT'S NAME:

APPLICANT'S BUSINESS ADDRESS: _____
(Display address exactly as it
should appear on registration) _____
_____

APPLICANT'S ENTITY TYPE: (Check one and supply requested information)

Individual - Citizen of (Country):
Partnership - State where organized (Country, if appropriate): _____   Names and Citizenship (Country) of General Partners:_____
Corporation - State (Country, if appropriate) of Incorporation: _____
Other (Specify Nature of Entity and Domicile): _____

Applicant requests registration of the certification mark shown in the accompanying drawing in the United States Patent and Trademark Office on the Principal Register established by the Act of July 5, 1946 (15 U.S.C. 1051 et. seq., as amended.) for the following goods/services (SPECIFIC GOODS AND/OR SERVICES MUST BE INSERTED HERE): _____
_____

The certification mark, as used (or, if filing under 15 U.S.C. 1051(b), intended to be used) by authorized persons, certifies (or, if filing under 15 U.S.C. 1051(b), is intended to certify): _____

(for example, a particular regional origin of the goods, a characteristic of the goods or services, that labor was performed by a particular group)

BASIS FOR APPLICATION: (Check boxes which apply, but never both the first AND second boxes, and supply requested information related to each box checked)

[ ]	Applicant is exercising legitimate control over the use of the certification mark in commerce on or in connection with the above-identified goods/services. (15 U.S.C. 1051(a) and 1054, as amended.) Three specimens showing the mark as used by authorized persons in commerce are submitted with this application. •Date of first use of the mark by authorized person in commerce which the U.S. Congress may regulate (for example, interstate or between the U.S. and a specified foreign country):_____ •Specify the type of commerce:_____ (for example, interstate or between the U.S. and a specified foreign country) •Date of first use anywhere by an authorized person (the same as or before use in commerce date): •Specify manner of using mark on or in connection with the goods/services: _____ (for example, mark is applied to labels for goods or mark is used on advertisements for services)
[ ]	Applicant has a bona fide intention to exercise legitimate control over the use of the certification mark in commerce on or in connection with the above-identified goods/services. (15 U.S.C. 1051(b) and 1054, as amended.) •Specify intended manner of using mark on or in connection with the goods/services: _____ (for example, mark will be applied to labels for goods or mark will be used on advertisements for services)
[ ]	Applicant has a bona fide intention to exercise legitimate control over the use of the certification mark in commerce on or in connection with the above-identified goods/services, and asserts a claim of priority based upon a foreign application in accordance with 15 U.S.C. 1126(d), as amended. • Country of foreign filing: _____ • Date of foreign filing: _____
[ ]	Applicant has a bona fide intention to exercise legitimate control over the use of the certification mark in commerce on or in connection with the above-identified goods/services and, accompanying this application, submits a certification or certified copy of a foreign registration in accordance with 15 U.S.C. 1126(e), as amended. • Country of registration: _____ • Registration number: _____

PTO FORM 4.9   U.S. DEPARTMENT OF COMMERCE/Patent and Trademark Office
OMB 0651-0009 (Exp. 6/30/92)

Applicant is not engaged (or, if filing under 15 U.S.C. 1051(b), will not engage) in the production or marketing of the goods or services to which the mark is applied.

The applicant must also provide a copy of the standards the applicant uses to determine whether goods or services will be certified. If the applicant files based on prior use in commerce, this should be provided with this application. In an application filed based on an intent to use in commerce, this should be provided with the Amendment to Allege Use or Statement or Use.

DECLARATION

The undersigned being hereby warned that willful false statements and the like so made are punishable by fine or imprisonment, or both, under 18 U.S.C. 1001, and that such willful false statements may jeopardize the validity of the application or any resulting registration, declares that he/she is properly authorized to execute this application on behalf of the applicant; he/she believes the applicant to be the owner of the mark sought to be registered, or, if the application is being filed under 15 U.S. 1051(b), he/she believes applicant is entitled to exercise legitimate control over use of the mark in commerce; to the best of his/her knowledge and belief no other person, firm, corporation, or association has the right to use the above identified mark in commerce, either in the identical form thereof or in such near resemblance thereto as to be likely, when used on or in connection with the goods/services of such other person, to cause confusion, or to cause mistake, or to deceive; and that all statements made of his/her own knowledge are true and that all statements made on information and belief are believed to be true.

_____   _____
Date   Signature

_____   _____
Telephone Number   Print or Type Name and Position

INSTRUCTIONS AND INFORMATION FOR APPLICANT

TO RECEIVE A FILING DATE, THE APPLICATION **MUST** BE COMPLETED AND SIGNED BY THE APPLICANT AND SUBMITTED ALONG WITH:

1. The prescribed FEE ($210.00) for each class of goods/services listed in the application;
2. A DRAWING PAGE displaying the mark in conformance with 37 CFR 2.52;
3. If the application is based on use of the mark in commerce, THREE (3) SPECIMENS (evidence) of the mark as used by authorized persons in commerce. All three specimens may be the same and may be in the nature of: (a) labels showing the mark which are placed on the goods; (b) photographs of the mark as it appears on the goods, (c) brochures or advertisements showing the mark as used in connection with the services.
4. An APPLICATION WITH DECLARATION (this form) - The application must be signed in order for the application to receive a filing date. Only the following person may sign the declaration, depending on the applicant's legal entity: (a) the individual applicant; (b) an officer of the corporate applicant; (c) one general partner of a partnership applicant; (d) all joint applicants.

SEND APPLICATION FORM, DRAWING PAGE, FEE, AND SPECIMENS (IF APPROPRIATE) TO:

U.S. DEPARTMENT OF COMMERCE
Patent and Trademark Office
Washington, D.C. 20231

Additional information concerning the requirements for filing an application is available in a booklet entitled Basic Facts About Trademarks, which may be obtained by writing to the above address or by calling: (703) 305-HELP.

This form is estimated to take an average of 1 hour to complete, including time required for reading and understanding instructions, gathering necessary information recordkeeping, and actually providing the information. Any comments on this form, including the amount of time required to complete this form, should be sent to the Office of Management and Organization, U.S. Patent and Trademark Office, U.S. Department of Commerce, Washington, D.C. 20231, and to Paperwork Reduction Project 0651-0009, Office of Information and Regulatory Affairs, Office of Management and Budget, Washington, D.C. 20503. Do NOT send completed forms to either of these addresses.

Appendix Four

Sample Trademark Drawing (Typed)

SAMPLE DRAWING - TYPEWRITTEN

8½" x 11" (21.6 cm x 27.9 cm)

APPLICANT'S NAME: A-OK Software Development Group

APPLICANT'S ADDRESS: 100 Main Street, Any town, MO 12345

GOODS: Computer software for analyzing statistics.

DATE OF FIRST USE: Intent-to-Use Application

DATE OF FIRST USE IN COMMERCE: Intent-to-Use Application

THEORYTEC

Appendix Five

Sample Trademark Drawing (Special Form)

SAMPLE DRAWING - SPECIAL FORM

8½" x 11" (21.6 cm x 27.9 cm)

APPLICANT'S NAME: Pinstripes Inc.

APPLICANT'S ADDRESS: 100 Main Street, Any town, MO 12345

GOODS AND SERVICES: Magazines in the field of business
management; business management
consulting services

FIRST USE: Magazines (Class 16) January 15, 1992
Consulting (Class 35) August 27, 1990

FIRST USE IN COMMERCE: Magazines (Class 16) January 15, 1992
Consulting (Class 35) August 27, 1990

DESIGN: A zebra

Appendix Six

Color Codes

THE DRAWING PAGE

Every application must include a single drawing page. If there is no drawing page, the application will be denied a filing date and returned to the applicant. The PTO uses the drawing to file the mark in the PTO search records and to print the mark in the Official Gazette and on the registration.

The drawing must be on pure white, durable, non-shiny paper that is 8½ (21.59 cm) inches wide by 11 (27.94 cm) inches long. There must be at least a one-inch (2.54 cm) margin on the sides, top and bottom of the page, and at least one inch between the heading and the display of the mark.

At the top of the drawing there must be a heading, listing on separate lines, the applicant's complete name, address, the goods and services specified in the application, and in applications based on use in commerce, the date of first use of the mark and the date of first use of the mark in commerce. This heading should be typewritten. If the drawing is in special form, the heading should include a description of the essential elements of the mark.

The drawing of the mark should appear at the center of the page. The drawing of the mark may be typewritten, as shown on page 19, or it may be in special form, as shown on page 18.

If the mark includes words, numbers or letters, the applicant can usually elect to submit either a typewritten or a special-form drawing. To register a mark consisting of only words, letters or numbers, without indicating any particular style or design, provide a typewritten drawing. In a typewritten drawing the mark must be typed entirely in CAPITAL LETTERS, even if the mark, as used, includes lower-case letters. Use a standard typewriter or type of the same size and style as that on a standard typewriter.

To indicate color, use the color linings shown below. The appropriate lining should appear in the area where the relevant color would appear. If the drawings is lined for color, insert a statement in the written application to indicate so, for example, "The mark is lined for the colors red and green." A plain black-and-white drawing is acceptable even if the mark is used in color. Most drawings do not indicate specific colors.

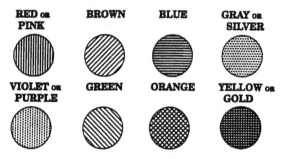

| **RED** or **PINK** | **BROWN** | **BLUE** | **GRAY** or **SILVER** |

| **VIOLET** or **PURPLE** | **GREEN** | **ORANGE** | **YELLOW** or **GOLD** |

Be careful in preparing the drawing. While it may be possible to make some minor changes, the rules prohibit any material change to the drawing of the mark after filing.

Appendix Seven

Statement of Use
With Declaration

STATEMENT OF USE UNDER 37 CFR 2.88, WITH DECLARATION	MARK (Identify the mark)
	SERIAL NO.

TO THE ASSISTANT SECRETARY AND COMMISSIONER OF PATENTS AND TRADEMARKS:

APPLICANT NAME:

NOTICE OF ALLOWANCE ISSUE DATE:

Applicant requests registration of the above-identified trademark/service mark in the United States Patent and Trademark Office on the Principal Register established by the Act of July 5, 1946 (15 U.S.C. 1051 et. seq., as amended). Three (3) specimens showing the mark as used in commerce are submitted with this statement.

☐   Check here only if a Request to Divide under 37 CFR 2.87 is being submitted with this Statement.

Applicant is using the mark in commerce on or in connection with the following goods/services: (Check One)

☐   Those goods/services identified in the Notice of Allowance in this application.

☐   Those goods/services identified in the Notice of Allowance in this application except: (Identify
     goods/services to be deleted from application)   _____

_____

_____

Date of first use of mark anywhere: _____

Date of first use of mark in commerce
which the U.S. Congress may regulate: _____

Specify type of commerce: (e.g., interstate, between the U.S. and a specified foreign country) _____

Specify manner or mode of use of mark on or in connection with the goods/services: (e.g., trademark is applied to labels, service mark is used in advertisements) _____

_____

The undersigned being hereby warned that willful false statements and the like so made are punishable by fine or imprisonment, or both, under 18 U.S.C. 1001, and that such willful false statements may jeopardize the validity of the application or any resulting registration, declares that he/she is properly authorized to execute this Statement of Use on behalf of the applicant; he/she believes the applicant to be the owner of the trademark/service mark sought to be registered; the trademark/ service mark is now in use in commerce; and all statements made of his/her own knowledge are true and all statements made on information and belief are believed to be true.

Date	Signature
Telephone Number	Print or Type Name and Position

PTO Form 1580 (REV. 6-92)
OMB No. 0651-0009
Exp. 6-30-95

U.S. DEPARTMENT OF COMMERCE/Patent and Trademark Office

209

INSTRUCTIONS AND INFORMATION FOR APPLICANT

In an application based upon a bona fide intention to use a mark in commerce, applicant must use its mark in commerce before a registration will be issued. After use begins, the applicant must submit, along with evidence of use (specimens) and the prescribed fee(s), either:

(1) an Amendment to Allege Use under 37 CFR 2.76, or
(2) a Statement of Use under 37 CFR 2.88.

The difference between these two filings is the timing of the filing. Applicant may file an Amendment to Allege Use before approval of the mark for publication for opposition in the Official Gazette, or, if a final refusal has been issued, prior to the expiration of the six month response period. Otherwise, applicant must file a Statement of Use after the Office issues a Notice of Allowance. The Notice of Allowance will issue after the opposition period is completed if no successful opposition is filed. Neither Amendment to Allege Use or Statement of Use papers will be accepted by the Office during the period of time between approval of the mark for publication for opposition in the Official Gazette and the issuance of the Notice of Allowance.

Applicant may call (703) 305-8747 to determine whether the mark has been approved for publication for opposition in the Official Gazette.

Before filing an Amendment to Allege Use or a Statement of Use, applicant must use the mark in commerce on or in connection with all of the goods/services for which applicant will seek registration, unless applicant submits with the papers, a request to divide out from the application the goods or services to which the Amendment to Allege Use or Statement of Use pertains. (See: 37 CFR 2.87, Dividing an application)

Applicant must submit with an Amendment to Allege Use or a Statement of Use:

(1) the appropriate fee of $100 per class of goods/services listed in the Amendment to Allege Use or the Statement of Use, and

(2) three (3) specimens or facsimiles of the mark as used in commerce for each class of goods/services asserted (e.g., photograph of mark as it appears on goods, label containing mark which is placed on goods, or brochure or advertisement showing mark as used in connection with services).

Cautions/Notes concerning completion of this Statement of Use form:

(1) The goods/services identified in the Statement of Use must be identical to the goods/services identified in the Notice of Allowance. Applicant may delete goods/services. Deleted goods/services may not be reinstated in the application at a later time.

(2) Applicant may list dates of use for only one item in each class of goods/services identified in the Statement of Use. However, applicant must have used the mark in commerce on all the goods/services in the class. Applicant must identify the particular item to which the dates apply.

(3) Only the following person may sign the verification of the Statement of Use, depending on the applicant's legal entity: (a) the individual applicant; (b) an officer of corporate applicant; (c) one general partner of partnership applicant; (d) all joint applicants.

MAIL COMPLETED FORM TO:

COMMISSIONER OF PATENTS AND TRADEMARKS
BOX ITU
WASHINGTON D.C. 20231

This form is estimated to take 15 minutes to complete including time required for reading and understanding instructions, gathering necessary information, record keeping and actually providing the information. Any comments on the amount of time you require to complete this form should be sent to the Office of Management and Organization, U.S. Patent and Trademark Office, U.S. Department of Commerce, Washington D.C., 20231, and to the Office of Information and Regulatory Affairs, Office of Management and Budget, Washington, D.C. 20503. Do not send completed form to OMB.

Appendix Eight

Amendment to Allege Use, With Declaration

AMENDMENT TO ALLEGE USE UNDER 37 CFR 2.76, WITH DECLARATION	MARK (Identify the mark)
	SERIAL NO.

TO THE ASSISTANT SECRETARY AND COMMISSIONER OF PATENTS AND TRADEMARKS:

APPLICANT NAME:

Applicant requests registration of the above-identified trademark/service mark in the United States Patent and Trademark Office on the Principal Register established by the Act of July 5, 1946 (15 U.S.C. 1051 et. seq., as amended). Three specimens showing the mark as used in commerce are submitted with this amendment.

☐   Check here if Request to Divide under 37 CFR 2.87 is being submitted with this amendment.

Applicant is using the mark in commerce on or in connection with the following goods/services:

_____

_____

(NOTE: Goods/services listed above may not be broader than the goods/services identified in the application as filed)

Date of first use of mark anywhere: _____

Date of first use of mark in commerce
which the U.S. Congress may regulate: _____

Specify type of commerce: (e.g., interstate, between the U.S. and a specified foreign country) _____

Specify manner or mode of use of mark on or in connection with the goods/services: (e.g., trademark is applied to labels, service mark is used in advertisements) _____

The undersigned being hereby warned that willful false statements and the like so made are punishable by fine or imprisonment, or both, under 18 U.S.C. 1001, and that such willful false statements may jeopardize the validity of the application or any resulting registration, declares that he/she is properly authorized to execute this Amendment to Allege Use on behalf of the applicant; he/she believes the applicant to be the owner of the trademark/service mark sought to be registered; the trademark/ service mark is now in use in commerce; and all statements made of his/her own knowledge are true and all statements made on information and belief are believed to be true.

Date	Signature
Telephone Number	Print or Type Name and Position

PTO Form 1579 (REV. 6-92)
OMB No. 0651-0009
Exp. 6-30-95

U.S. DEPARTMENT OF COMMERCE/Patent and Trademark Office

211

INSTRUCTIONS AND INFORMATION FOR APPLICANT

In an application based upon a bona fide intention to use a mark in commerce, applicant must use its mark in commerce before a registration will be issued. After use begins, the applicant must submit, along with evidence of use (specimens) and the prescribed fee(s), **either:**

(1) an Amendment to Allege Use under 37 CFR 2.76, or
(2) a Statement of Use under 37 CFR 2.88.

The difference between these two filings is the timing of the filing. Applicant may file an Amendment to Allege Use before approval of the mark for publication for opposition in the **Official Gazette**, or, if a final refusal has been issued, prior to the expiration of the six month response period. Otherwise, applicant must file a Statement of Use after the Office issues a Notice of Allowance. The Notice of Allowance will issue after the opposition period is completed if no successful opposition is filed. Neither Amendment to Allege Use or Statement of Use papers will be accepted by the Office during the period of time between approval of the mark for publication for opposition in the **Official Gazette** and the issuance of the Notice of Allowance.

Applicant may call (703) 305-8747 to determine whether the mark has been approved for publication for opposition in the **Official Gazette.**

Before filing an Amendment to Allege Use or a Statement of Use, applicant must use the mark in commerce on or in connection with **all** of the goods/services for which applicant will seek registration, **unless** applicant submits with the papers, a request to divide out from the application the goods or services to which the Amendment to Allege Use or Statement of Use pertains. (See: 37 CFR 2.87, Dividing an application)

Applicant **must** submit with an Amendment to Allege Use or a Statement of Use:

(1) the appropriate fee of $100 per class of goods/services listed in the Amendment to Allege Use or the Statement of Use, and

(2) three (3) specimens or facsimiles of the mark as used in commerce for each class of goods/services asserted (e.g., photograph of mark as it appears on goods, label containing mark which is placed on goods, or brochure or advertisement showing mark as used in connection with services).

Cautions/Notes concerning completion of this Amendment to Allege Use form:

(1) The goods/services identified in the Amendment to Allege Use must be within the scope of the goods/services identified in the application as filed. Applicant may delete goods/services. Deleted goods/services may not be reinstated in the application at a later time.

(2) Applicant may list dates of use for only one item in each class of goods/services identified in the Amendment to Allege Use. However, applicant must have used the mark in commerce on all the goods/services in the class.

(3) Only the following person may sign the verification of the Amendment to Allege Use, depending on the applicant's legal entity: (a) the individual applicant; (b) an officer of corporate applicant; (c) one general partner of partnership applicant; (d) all joint applicants.

MAIL COMPLETED FORM TO:

**COMMISSIONER OF PATENTS AND TRADEMARKS
WASHINGTON, D.C. 20231**

This form is estimated to take 15 minutes to complete including time required for reading and understanding instructions, gathering necessary information, record keeping and actually providing the information. Any comments on the amount of time you require to complete this form should be sent to the Office of Management and Organization, U.S. Patent and Trademark Office, U.S. Department of Commerce, Washington D.C., 20231, and to the Office of Information and Regulatory Affairs, Office of Management and Budget, Washington, D.C. 20503. Do not send completed from to OMB.

Appendix Nine

Request for Extension of Time to File a Statement of Use, With Declaration

REQUEST FOR EXTENSION OF TIME UNDER 37 CFR 2.89 TO FILE A STATEMENT OF USE, WITH DECLARATION	MARK (Identify the mark)
	SERIAL NO.

TO THE ASSISTANT SECRETARY AND COMMISSIONER OF PATENTS AND TRADEMARKS:

APPLICANT NAME:

NOTICE OF ALLOWANCE MAILING DATE:

Applicant requests a six-month extension of time to file the Statement of Use under 37 CFR 2.88 in this application.

☐   Check here if a Request to Divide under 37 CFR 2.87 is being submitted with this request.

Applicant has a continued bona fide intention to use the mark in commerce in connection with the following goods/services: (Check one below)

☐   Those goods/services identified in the Notice of Allowance in this application.

☐   Those goods/services identified in the Notice of Allowance in this application except: (Identify goods/services to be deleted from application) _____

This is the _____ request for an Extension of Time following mailing of the Notice of Allowance.
        (Specify: First - Fifth)

If this is not the first request for an Extension of Time, check one box below. If the first box is checked, explain the circumstance(s) of the non-use in the space provided:

☐   Applicant has not used the mark in commerce yet on all goods/services specified in the Notice of Allowance; however, applicant has made the following ongoing efforts to use the mark in commerce on or in connection with each of the goods/services specified above:

_____

If additional space is needed, please attach a separate sheet to this form

☐   Applicant believes that it has made valid use of the mark in commerce, as evidenced by the Statement of Use submitted with this request; however, if the Statement of Use does not meet minimum requirements under 37 CFR 2.88(e), applicant will need additional time in which to file a new statement.

The undersigned being hereby warned that willful false statements and the like so made are punishable by fine or imprisonment, or both, under 18 U.S.C. 1001, and that such willful false statements may jeopardize the validity of the application or any resulting registration, declares that he/she is properly authorized to execute this Request for Extension of Time to File a Statement of Use on behalf of the applicant; he/she believes the applicant to be entitled to use the trademark/service mark sought to be registered; and all statements made of his/her own knowledge are true and all statements made on information and belief are believed to be true.

Date _____   Signature _____

Telephone Number _____   Print or Type Name and Position _____

PTO Form 1581 (REV. 6-92)
OMB No. 0651 - 0009
Exp. 6-30-95

U.S. DEPARTMENT OF COMMERCE/Patent and Trademark Office

INSTRUCTIONS AND INFORMATION FOR APPLICANT

Applicant must file a Statement of Use within six months after the mailing of the Notice of Allowance in an application based upon a bona fide intention to use a mark in commerce, UNLESS, within that same period, applicant submits a request for a six-month extension of time to file the Statement of Use. The request must:

(1) be in writing,
(2) include applicant's verified statement of continued bona fide intention to use the mark in commerce,
(3) specify the goods/services to which the request pertains as they are identified in the Notice of Allowance, and
(4) include a fee of $100 for each class of goods/services.

Applicant may request four further six-month extensions of time. No extension may extend beyond 36 months from the issue date of the Notice of Allowance. Each request must be filed within the previously granted six-month extension period and must include, in addition to the above requirements, a showing of GOOD CAUSE. This good cause showing must include:

(1) applicant's statement that the mark has not been used in commerce yet on all the goods or services specified in the Notice of Allowance with which applicant has a continued bona fide intention to use the mark in commerce, and

(2) applicant's statement of ongoing efforts to make such use, which may include the following: (a) product or service research or development, (b) market research,
(c) promotional activities, (d) steps to acquire distributors, (e) steps to obtain required governmental approval, or (f) similar specified activity .

Applicant may submit one additional six-month extension request during the existing period in which applicant files the Statement of Use, unless the granting of this request would extend beyond 36 months from the issue date of the Notice of Allowance. As a showing of good cause, applicant should state its belief that applicant has made valid use of the mark in commerce, as evidenced by the submitted Statement of Use, but that if the Statement is found by the PTO to be defective, applicant will need additional time in which to file a new statement of use.

Only the following person may sign the verification of the Request for Extentsion of Time, depending on the applicant's legal entity: (a) the individual applicant; (b) an officer of corporate applicant; (c) one general partner of partnership applicant; (d) all joint applicants.

MAIL COMPLETED FORM TO:

**COMMISSIONER OF PATENTS & TRADEMARKS
BOX ITU
WASHINGTON, D.C. 20231**

This form is estimated to take 15 minutes to complete including time required for reading and understanding instructions, gathering necessary information, record keeping and actually providing the information. Any comments on the amount of time you require to complete this form should be sent to the Office of Management and Organization, U.S. Patent and Trademark Office, U.S. Department of Commerce, Washington D.C., 20231, and to the Office of Information and Regulatory Affairs, Office of Management and Budget, Washington, D.C. 20503. Do not send completed form to OMB

Appendix Ten

Suggested Format for Notice of Opposition

IN THE UNITED STATES PATENT AND TRADEMARK OFFICE
BEFORE THE TRADEMARK TRIAL AND APPEAL BOARD

In the matter of trademark application Serial No._____

Filed _____
For the mark _____
Published in the Official Gazette on _____
                                        (Date)

_____
(Name of Opposer)

v.

_____
(Name of Applicant)

Opposition No. _____
             (To be inserted by Patent & Trademark Office)

NOTICE OF OPPOSITION
(State opposer's name, address, and entity information)[1]

_____
(Name of individual as opposer, and business trade name, if any)

_____
(Business Address)

OR _____
             (Name of partnership as opposer)

_____
(Names of partners)

_____
(Business address of partnership)

OR
_____

(Name of corporation as opposer)

_____

(State or country of incorporation)

_____

(Business address of corporation)

The above-identified opposer believes that it/he/she will be damaged by registration of the mark shown in the above-identified application, and hereby opposes the same.[2]
The grounds for opposition are as follows:[3]

By _____

(Signature)[4]

_____

(Identification of person signing)[5]

REPRESENTATION INFORMATION

If the opposer is not domiciled in the United States, and is not represented by an attorney or other authorized representative located in the United States, a domestic representative must be designated.

If the opposer wishes to furnish a power of attorney, it may do so, but an attorney at law is not required to furnish a power.

_____

[1] If opposer is an individual, state the opposer's name, business trade name, if any, and business address. If opposer is a partnership, state the name of the partnership, the names of the partners, and the business address of the partnership. If opposer is a corporation, state the name of the corporation, the state (or country, if opposer is a foreign corporation) of incorporation, and the business address of the corporation. If opposer is an association or other similar type of juristic entity, state the information required for a corporation, changing the term "corporation" throughout to an appropriate designation.

[2] The required fee must be submitted for each party joined as opposer for each class opposed, and if fewer than the total number of classes

in the application are opposed, the classes opposed should be specified.

[3] Set forth a short and plain statement here showing why the opposer believes it/he/she would be damaged by the registration of the opposed mark, and state the grounds for opposing.

[4] The opposition need not be verified, and may be signed by the opposer or by the opposer's attorney or other authorized representative. If an opposer signing for itself is a partnership, the signature must be made by a partner; if an opposer signing for itself is a corporation or similar juristic entity, the signature must be made by an officer of the corporation or other juristic entity who has authority to sign for the entity and whose title is given.

[5] State the capacity in which the signing individual signs, e.g., attorney for opposer, opposer (if opposer is an individual), partner of opposer (if opposer is a partnership), officer of opposer identified by title (if opposer is a corporation), etc.

Appendix Eleven

Suggested Format for Petition to Cancel

IN THE UNITED STATES PATENT AND TRADEMARK OFFICE BEFORE THE TRADEMARK TRIAL AND APPEAL BOARD

In the matter of trademark Registration No _____

For the mark _____

Date registered _____

_____

(Name of petitioner)

v.

_____

(Name of registrant)

Cancellation No. _____

(To be inserted by Patent and Trademark Office)

PETITION TO CANCEL
(State petitioner's name, address, and entity information)[1]

_____

(Name of individual as petitioner, and business trade name, if any)

_____

(Business Address)

OR _____

(Name of partnership as petitioner)

_____

(Names of partners)

_____

(Business address of partnership)

OR _____

(Name of corporation as petitioner)

_____

(State or country of incorporation)

(Business address of corporation)

To the best of petitioner's knowledge, the name and address of the current owner of the registration are _____

The above-identified petitioner believes that it/he/she will be damaged by the above-identified registration, and hereby petitions to cancel the same.[2]
The grounds for cancellation are as follows:[3]

By _____
    (Signature)[4]

(Identification of person signing)[5]

REPRESENTATION INFORMATION

If the petitioner is not domiciled in the United States, and is not represented by an attorney or other authorized representative located in the United States, a domestic representative must be designated.

If a petitioner wishes to furnish a power of attorney, it may do so, but an attorney at law is not required to furnish a power.

---

[1] If petitioner is an individual, state the petitioner's name, business trade name, if any, and business address. If petitioner is a partnership, state the name of the partnership, the names of the partners, and the business address of the partnership. If petitioner is a corporation, state the name of the corporation, the state (or country, if petitioner is a foreign corporation) of incorporation, and the business address of the corporation. If petitioner is an association or other similar type of juristic entity, state the information required for a corporation, changing the term "corporation" throughout to an appropriate designation.

[2] The required fee must be submitted for each party joined as petitioner for each class sought to be canceled, and if cancellation is sought for fewer than the total number of classes in the registration, the classes sought to be canceled should be specified.

[3] Set forth a short and plain statement here showing why the petitioner believes it/he/she would be damaged by the registration, and state the grounds for cancellation.

[4] The petition need not be verified, and may be signed by the petitioner or by the petitioner's attorney or other authorized representative. If a petitioner signing for itself is a partnership, the signature must be made by a partner; if a petitioner signing for itself is a corporation or other juristic entity who has authority to sign for the entity and whose title is given.

[5] State the capacity in which the signing individual signs, e.g., attorney for petitioner, petitioner (if petitioner is an individual), partner of petitioner (if petitioner is a partnership), officer of petitioner identified by title (if petitioner is a corporation), etc.

Appendix Twelve

Combined Section 8 and 15 Declaration

COMBINED DECLARATION OF USE AND INCONTESTABILITY UNDER SECTIONS 8 & 15[1] OF THE TRADEMARK ACT OF 1946, AS AMENDED	MARK (Identify the mark)	
	REGISTRATION NO.	DATE OF REGISTRATION:

TO THE ASSISTANT SECRETARY AND COMMISSIONER OF PATENTS AND TRADEMARKS:

REGISTRANT'S NAME:[2]

REGISTRANT'S CURRENT MAILING ADDRESS: _____

_____

_____

GOODS AND/OR SERVICES AND USE IN COMMERCE STATEMENT:

The mark shown in Registration No. _____, owned by the above-identified registrant, has been in

continuous use in _____ commerce for five consecutive years from the date of registration or the
       (type of)[3]

date of publication under §12(c)[4] to the present, on or in connection with all of the goods and/or services

identified in the registration, (*except* for the following)[5] _____

_____

as evidenced by the attached specimen(s)[6] showing the mark as currently used. There has been no final

decision adverse to registrant's claim of ownership of such mark for such goods or services, or to registrant's

right to register the same or to keep the same on the register; and there is no proceeding involving said

rights pending and not disposed of either in the Patent and Trademark Office or in the courts.

DECLARATION

The undersigned being hereby warned that willful false statements and the like so made are punishable by fine or imprisonment, or both, under 18 U.S.C. 1001, and that such willful false statements may jeopardize the validity of this document, declares that he/she is properly authorized to execute this document on behalf of the registrant; he/she believes the registrant to be the owner of the above identified registration; the trademark/service mark is in use in commerce; and all statements made of his/her own knowledge are true and all statements made on information and belief are believed to be true.

_____   _____
Date   Signature

_____   _____
Telephone Number   Print or Type Name and Position
                                  [if applicable][7]

PTO-FB-TM (Combined 8 & 15) (Rev. 1/93)   U.S. DEPARTMENT OF COMMERCE/Patent and Trademark Office
OMB No. 0651-0009 (Exp. 6/30/95)

FOOTNOTES

1. If you do not have five years of continuous use, you should file a Section 8 affidavit only. Please see PTO Form #1583.

2. The present owner of the registration must file this form between the 5th and 6th year after registration. If ownership of the registration has changed since the registration date, provide supporting documentation if available or a verified explanation. The present owner should refer to itself as the registrant.

3. "Type of Commerce" must be specified as "interstate," "territorial," "foreign," or such other commerce as may lawfully be regulated by Congress. Foreign registrants must specify commerce which Congress may regulate, using wording such as "foreign commerce between the U.S. and a foreign country."

4. This combined form is only appropriate when the five year period of continuous use, which is required for Section 15, (1) occurs between the 5th and 6th year after registration, or (2) after publication under §12(c) as is required for Section 8.

5. List only those goods and/or services for which registrant is no longer using the mark. You should fill in this blank only if you are no longer using the mark on all the goods or services in the registration.

6. A specimen showing current use of the registered mark for at least one product or service in each class of the registration must be submitted with this form. Examples of specimens are tags or labels for goods, and advertisements for services.

7. If the present owner is an individual, the individual should sign the declaration.

    If the present owner is a partnership, the declaration should be signed by a General Partner.

    If the present owner is a corporation or similar juristic entity, the declaration should be signed by an officer of the corporation/entity. Please print or type the officer title of the person signing the declaration.

NOTE: If the registration is owned by more than one party, as joint owners, each owner must sign this declaration.

FEES

For each declaration under Sections 8 & 15, the required fee is $200.00 per international class. Please be aware that our fees may change. Changes, if any, are normally effective October 1 of each year. If this declaration is intended to cover less than the total number of classes in the registration, please specify the classes for which the declaration is submitted. The declaration, with appropriate fee(s), should be sent to:

Commissioner of Patents & Trademarks
Washington, D.C. 20231

MAILING INSTRUCTION BOX

You can ensure timely filing of this form by following the procedure described in 37 CFR 1.10 as follows: (1) on or before the due date for filing this form, deposit the completed form with the U.S. Post Office using the "Express Mail Post Office to Addressee" Service; (2) include a certificate of "Express Mail" under 37 CFR 1.10. Papers properly mailed under 37 CFR 1.10 are considered received by the PTO on the date that they are deposited with the Post Office.

When placing the certificate directly on the correspondence, use the following language:

Certificate of Express Mail Under 37 CFR 1.10

"Express Mail" mailing label number: _____
Date of Deposit: _____
I hereby certify that this paper and fee is being deposited with the United States Postal Service "Express Mail Post Office to Addressee" service under 37 CFR 1.10 on the date indicated above and is addressed to the Commissioner of Patents and Trademarks, Washington, D.C. 20231.

_____   _____
(Typed or printed name of person mailing   (Signature of person mailing paper & fee)
paper & fee)

This form is estimated to take 15 minutes to complete. Time will vary depending upon the needs of the individual case. Any comments on the amount of time you require to complete this form should be sent to the Office of Management and Organization, U.S. Patent and Trademark Office, U.S. Department of Commerce, Washington, D.C. 20231, and to the Office of Information and Regulatory Affairs, Office of Management and Budget, Washington, D.C. 20503. DO NOT SEND FORMS TO EITHER OF THESE ADDRESSES.

Appendix Thirteen

Application for Renewal

APPLICATION FOR RENEWAL OF REGISTRATION OF A MARK UNDER SECTION 9 OF THE TRADEMARK ACT OF 1946, AS AMENDED	MARK (Identify the mark)	
	REGISTRATION NO.	DATE OF REGISTRATION:

TO THE ASSISTANT SECRETARY AND COMMISSIONER OF PATENTS AND TRADEMARKS:

REGISTRANT'S NAME:[1]

REGISTRANT'S CURRENT MAILING ADDRESS: _____

GOODS AND/OR SERVICES AND USE IN COMMERCE STATEMENT:

The mark shown in Registration No. _____ owned by the above-identified registrant is still in use

in _____ commerce on or in connection with all of the goods and/or services identified in the
(type of)[2]

registration, (*except* for the following)[3] _____

as evidenced by the attached specimen(s)[4] showing the mark as currently used.

DECLARATION

The undersigned being hereby warned that willful false statements and the like so made are punishable by fine or imprisonment, or both, under 18 U.S.C. 1001, and that such willful false statements may jeopardize the validity of this document, declares that he/she is properly authorized to execute this document on behalf of the registrant; he/she believes the registrant to be the owner of the above identified registration; the trademark/service mark is in use in commerce; and all statements made of his/her own knowledge are true and all statements made on information and belief are believed to be true.

_____
Date

_____
Signature

_____
Telephone Number

_____
Print or Type Name and Position
[if applicable][5]

PTO Form 4.13a (Rev. 1/93)   U.S. DEPARTMENT OF COMMERCE/Patent and Trademark Office
OMB No. 0651-0009 (Exp. 6/30/95)

FOOTNOTES

1. The present owner of the registration must file this form within 6 months prior to the expiration of the registration term. The form may also be filed within a 3 month grace period following the expiration of the registration term upon payment of the late fee. If ownership of the registration has changed since the registration date, provide supporting documentation if available or a verified explanation. The present owner should refer to itself as the registrant.

2. "Type of Commerce" must be specified as "interstate," "territorial," "foreign," or such other commerce as may lawfully be regulated by Congress. Foreign registrants must specify commerce which Congress may regulate, using wording such as "foreign commerce between the U.S. and a foreign country."

3. List only those goods and/or services for which registrant is no longer using the mark. You should fill in this blank only if you are no longer using the mark on all the goods or services in the registration.

4. A specimen showing current use of the registered mark for at least one product or service in each class of the registration must be submitted with this form. Examples of specimens are tags or labels for goods, and advertisements for services.

5. If the present owner is an individual, the individual should sign the declaration.

   If the present owner is a partnership, the declaration should be signed by a General Partner.

   If the present owner is a corporation or similar juristic entity, the declaration should be signed by an officer of the corporation/entity. Please print or type the officer title of the person signing the declaration.

NOTE: If the registration is owned by more than one party, as joint owners, each owner must sign this declaration.

FEES

For each renewal application under Section 9, the required fee is $300.00 per class. Please be aware that our fees may change. Changes, if any, are normally effective October 1 of each year. If filed during the three month grace period a late fee of $100.00 per class must also be submitted. If this renewal application is intended to cover less than the total number of classes in the registration, please specify the classes for which the renewal application is submitted. The renewal application, with appropriate fee(s), should be sent to:

Commissioner of Patents & Trademarks
Washington, D.C. 20231

MAILING INSTRUCTION BOX

You can ensure timely filing of this form by following the procedure described in 37 CFR 1.10 as follows: (1) on or before the due date for filing this form, deposit the completed form with the U.S. Post Office using the "Express Mail Post Office to Addressee" Service; (2) include a certificate of "Express Mail" under 37 CFR 1.10. Papers properly mailed under 37 CFR 1.10 are considered received by the PTO on the date that they are deposited with the Post Office.

When placing the certificate directly on the correspondence, use the following language:

   Certificate of Express Mail Under 37 CFR 1.10

   "Express Mail" mailing label number: _____
   Date of Deposit: _____
   I hereby certify that this paper and fee is being deposited with the United States Postal Service "Express Mail Post Office to Addressee" service under 37 CFR 1.10 on the date indicated above and is addressed to the Commissioner of Patents and Trademarks, Washington, D.C. 20231.

   _____   _____
   (Typed or printed name of person mailing   (Signature of person mailing paper & fee)
   paper & fee)

This form is estimated to take 15 minutes to complete. Time will vary depending upon the needs of the individual case. Any comments on the amount of time you require to complete this form should be sent to the Office of Management and Organization, U.S. Patent and Trademark Office, U.S. Department of Commerce, Washington, D.C. 20231, and to the Office of Information and Regulatory Affairs, Office of Management and Budget, Washington, D.C. 20503. DO NOT SEND FORMS TO EITHER OF THESE ADDRESSES.

Appendix Fourteen

Assignment Recordal Form

FORM PTO-1594 1-31-92	RECORDATION FORM COVER SHEET **TRADEMARKS ONLY**	U.S. DEPARTMENT OF COMMERCE Patent and Trademark Office

Tab settings ◑ ◑ ◑ ▼   ▼   ▼   ▼   ▼   ▼

To the Honorable Commissioner of Patents and Trademarks: Please record the attached original documents or copy thereof.

1. Name of conveying party(ies):

2. Name and address of receiving party(ies):

Name: _____

Internal Address: _____

Street Address: _____

☐ Individual(s)   ☐ Association
☐ General Partnership   ☐ Limited Partnership
☐ Corporation-State
☐ Other _____

Additional name(s) of conveying party(ies) attached? ☐ Yes ☐ No

City: _____ State: _____ ZIP: _____

☐ Individual(s) citizenship _____
☐ Association _____
☐ General Partnership _____
☐ Limited Partnership _____
☐ Corporation-State _____
☐ Other _____

3. Nature of conveyance:

☐ Assignment   ☐ Merger
☐ Security Agreement   ☐ Change of Name
☐ Other _____

Execution Date: _____

If assignee is not domiciled in the United States, a domestic representative designation is attached: ☐ Yes ☐ No
(Designations must be a separate document from Assignment)
Additional name(s) & address(es) attached? ☐ Yes ☐ No

4. Application number(s) or registration number(s):

A. Trademark Application No.(s)

B. Trademark registration No.(s)

Additional numbers attached? ☐ Yes ☐ No

5. Name and address of party to whom correspondence concerning document should be mailed:

Name: _____

Internal Address: _____

Street Address: _____

City: _____ State: _____ ZIP: _____

6. Total number of applications and registrations involved: .... [ ]

7. Total fee (37 CFR 3.41) .... $ _____

☐ Enclosed

☐ Authorized to be charged to deposit account

8. Deposit account number: _____

(Attach duplicate copy of this page if paying by deposit account)

DO NOT USE THIS SPACE

9. Statement and signature.
To the best of my knowledge and belief, the foregoing information is true and correct and any attached copy is a true copy of the original document.

_____   _____   _____
Name of Person Signing   Signature   Date

Total number of pages comprising cover sheet: [ ]

OMB No. 0651-0011 (exp. 4/94)

- -

Do not detach this portion

Mail documents to be recorded with required cover sheet information to:

**Commissioner of Patents and Trademarks
Box Assignments
Washington, D.C. 20231**

Public burden reporting for this sample cover sheet is estimated to average about 30 minutes per document to be recorded, including time for reviewing the document and gathering the data needed,, and completing and reviewing the sample cover sheet. Send comments regarding this burden estimate to the U.S. Patent and Trademark Office, Office of Information Systems, PK2-1000C, Washington, D.C. 20231, and to the Office of Management and Budget, Paperwork Reduction Project (0651-0011), Washington, D.C. 20503.

Appendix Fifteen

List of Patent and Trademark Depository Libraries

The following libraries, designated as Patent and Trademark Depository Libraries (PTDLs) receive patent and trademark information in various formats from the U.S. Patent and Trademark Office. Many PTDLs have on file all full-text patents issued since 1790, trademarks published since 1872, and select collections of foreign patents. All PTDLs have both the patent and trademark sections of the *Official Gazette of the U.S. Patent and Trademark Office*. The full-text utility and design patents are distributed numerically on 16 mm microfilm, and plant patents on color microfiche. Patent and trademark search systems on CD-ROM format are available at all PTDLs to increase utilization of an enhance access to the information found in patents and trademarks. It is through the CD-ROM systems that preliminary patent and trademark searches can be conducted through the numerically arranged collections.

All information is available for use by the public free of charge. Facilities for making paper copies of patent and trademark information are generally provided for a fee.

State	Name of Library .... Telephone
Alabama	Auburn University Libraries 205-844-1747
	Birmingham Public Library 205-226-3520
Alaska	Anchorage: Z.J. Loussac Public Library 907-562-7323
Arizona	Tempe: Noble Library, Arizona State University 602-965-7010
Arkansas	Little Rock: Arkansas State Library 501-682-2053
California	Los Angeles Public Library 213-228-7220
	Sacramento: California State Library 916-654-0069
	San Diego Public Library 619-236-5813
	San Francisco Public Library .... Not Operational
	Sunny vale Patent Clearinghouse 408-730-7290
Colorado	Denver Public Library 303-640-8847
Connecticut	New Haven: Science Park Library 203-786-5447
Delaware	Newark: University of Delaware Library ... 302-831-2965
Dist. of Columbia	Washington: Howard University Libraries . 202-806-7252

Florida	Fort Lauderdale: Broward County	
	Main Library	305-357-7444
	Miami-Dade Public Library	305-375-2665
	Orlando: University of Central Florida	
	Libraries	407-823-2562
	Tampa: Tampa Campus Library, University	
	of South Florida	813-974-2726
Georgia	Atlanta: Price Gilbert Memorial Library,	
	Georgia Institute of Technology	404-894-4508
Hawaii	Honolulu: Hawaii State Public Library	
	System	808-586-3477
Idaho	Moscow: University of Idaho Library	208-885-6235
Illinois	Chicago Public Library	312-747-4450
	Springfield: Illinois State Library	217-782-5659
Indiana	Indianapolis-Marion County Public	
	Library	317-269-1741
	West Lafayette: Purdue University	
	Libraries	317-494-2873
Iowa	Des Moines: State Library of Iowa	515-281-4118
Kansas	Wichita: Ablah Library, Wichita State	
	University	316-689-3155
Kentucky	Louisville Free Public Library	502-574-1611
Louisiana	Baton Rouge: Troy H. Middleton Library,	
	Louisiana State University	504-388-2570
Maine	Orono: Raymond H. Fogler Library,	
	University of Maine	Not Operational
Maryland	College Park: Engineering and Physical	
	Sciences Library, University of Maryland	301-405-9157
Massachusetts	Amherst: Physical Sciences Library,	
	University of Massachusetts	413-545-1370
	Boston Public Library	617-536-5400 ext. 265
Michigan	Ann Arbor: Engineering Transportation Library,	
	University of Michigan	313-764-5298
	Big Rapids: Abigail S. Timme Library,	
	Ferris State University	616-592-3602
	Detroit Public Library	313-833-1450
Minnesota	Minneapolis Public Library and	
	Information Center	612-372-6570
Mississippi	Jackson: Mississippi Library Commission	601-359-1036
Missouri	Kansas City: Linda Hall Library	816-363-4600
	St. Louis Public Library	314-241-2288 ext. 390
Montana	Butte: Montana College of Mineral Science	
	and Technology Library	406-496-4281

Nebraska	Lincoln: Engineering Library, University of Nebraska-Lincoln 402-472-3411
Nevada	Reno: University of Nevada-Reno Library . 702-784-6579
New Hampshire	Durham: University of New Hampshire Library 603-862-1777
New Jersey	Newark Public Library 201-733-7782
	Piscataway: Library of Sciences and Medicine, Rutgers University 908-445-2895
New Mexico	Albuquerque: University of New Mexico General Library 505-277-4412
New York	Albany: New York State Library 518-474-5355
	Buffalo and Erie County Public Library 716-858-7101
	New York Public Library (The Research Libraries) 212-930-0917
North Carolina	Raleigh: D.H. Hill Library, North Carolina State University 919-515-3280
North Dakota	Grand Forks: Chester Fritz Library, University of North Dakota 701-777-4888
Ohio	Cincinnati and Hamilton County Public Library of 513-369-6936
	Cleveland Public Library 216-623-2870
	Columbus: Ohio State University Libraries 614-292-6175
	Toledo/Lucas County Public Library 419-259-5212
Oklahoma	Stillwater: Oklahoma State University Library 405-744-7086
Oregon	Salem: Oregon State Library 503-378-4239
Pennsylvania	Philadelphia, The Free Library of 215-686-5331
	Pittsburgh, Carnegie Library of 412-622-3138
	University Park: Library, Pennsylvania State University 814-865-4861
Rhode Island	Providence Public Library 401-455-8027
South Carolina	Charleston: Medical University of South Carolina Library 803-792-2372
	Clemson University Libraries 803-656-3024
South Dakota	Rapid City: Deveraux Library, South Dakota School of Mines and Technology .... Not Operational
Tennessee	Memphis & Shelby County Public Library and Information Center 901-725-8877
	Nashville: Stevenson Science Library, Vanderbilt University 615-322-2775
Texas	Austin: McKinney Engineering Library, University of Texas at Austin 512-495-4500
	College Station: Sterling C. Evans Library, Texas A&M University 409-845-3826

	Dallas Public Library 214-670-1468
	Houston: The Fondren Library,
	Rice University 713-527-8101
	ext. 2587
Utah	Salt Lake City: Marriott Library,
	University of Utah 801-581-8394
Virginia	Richmond: James Branch Cabell Library,
	Virginia Commonwealth University 804-828-1104
Washington	Seattle: Engineering Library,
	University of Washington............................. 206-543-0740
West Virginia	Morgantown: Evansdale Library,
	West Virginia University............................... 304-293-4510
Wisconsin	Madison: Kurt F. Wendt Library,
	University of Wisconsin Madison 608-262-6845
	Milwaukee Public Library 414-286-3247
Wyoming	Casper: Natrona County Public Library ..... Not Operational

Glossary

Abandonment — A trademark is deemed to be "abandoned" when either of the following occurs: (1) when its use has been discontinued with intent not to resume such use or (2) when any course of conduct of the owner, including acts of omission as well as commission, causes a mark to become the generic name for the goods or services on or in connection with which it is used, or otherwise to lose its significance as a mark. Non-use for three consecutive years is deemed prima facie evidence of abandonment. Use means ordinary use in the course of commerce and not use merely to reserve a right in the mark. Conduct by a trademark owner which causes a mark to lose its significance includes not policing the mark; assigning a trademark without goodwill; uncontrolled licensing; failure to object to use by others; production of various types and quality of products; and substantial and repeated changes in the mark. When a mark is abandoned, it enters the public domain and becomes available to the first user.

Applicant — A person who files an application for a federal trademark. The term embraces the legal representatives, predecessors, successors and assigns of such applicant. (See "Registrant.")

Cancellations — Cancellations are similar to oppositions, except that they are instituted post-registration. Frequently, an applicant brings a cancellation to remove a registration cited against a pending application based on alleged abandonment, prior use by the applicant or the mark being descriptive or generic. Actions based on descriptiveness or prior use cannot be brought after a registration becomes incontestable, i.e., after a Section 15 Declaration has been filed. However, even after a registration becomes incontestable, a cancellation based on the mark being generic or abandoned can be filed. Use by the petitioner before the filing date of the registrant, even only local use, will defeat the registration. Standing is required to bring a cancellation and a filing fee is required. (See Chapter Ten.)

Certification Mark — The term "certification mark" means any word, name, symbol, or any combination thereof– (1) used by a person other than the owner, or (2) which its owner has a bona fide intention to permit a person other than the owner to use in commerce and files an application to register on the Principal Register. The owner sets the standards for the members to follow. Examples are to certify regional or other origin, material, mode of manufacture, quality, accuracy, union labor, etc.

Collective Mark — The term "collective mark" means a trademark or service mark– (1) used by the members of a cooperative, an association, or other collective group or organization, or (2) which such cooperative, association, group, or organization has a bona fide intention to use in commerce and applies to register on the Principal Register.

Colorable Imitation — The term "colorable imitation" includes any mark which so resembles a registered mark as to be likely to cause confusion or mistake or to deceive.

Commerce — The word "commerce" means all commerce which may lawfully be regulated by Congress. No limitations can be read into this.

Common Law Rights — Common law trademarks and trade names are non-statutory, use-related rights, which result from selling a product under a trademark or providing a service under a service mark. These rights exist even though state and federal trademarks laws are now in force. When a trademarked product is sold, when services are performed under a service mark, or when a business is operated under a trade name, the owner or seller acquires rights to prevent others from using the same, or confusingly similar, marks or names, for similar goods and services or businesses in the same market territory.

Concurrent Use — Concurrent use is an inter partes proceeding where several parties are granted registrations for the same mark covering different parts of the country. The proceeding is instituted following publication of a mark for opposition and is conducted before the Board of Appeals. The first user or registrant is entitled to nationwide registration, subject to the second party's use area. These proceedings are much less common than oppositions.

Counterfeit — A counterfeit is a spurious mark which is identical with, or substantially indistinguishable from, a registered mark. Counterfeits are infringements, but counterfeits are also subject to criminal penalties and seizure. The Trademark Counterfeiting Act of 1984 provides criminal penalties up to $250,000 and/or five years imprisonment for intentional trafficking or attempted trafficking and knowing use of the counterfeit mark. Corporations can be fined up to $1,000,000. Civil remedies mandate treble damages or profits and attorney fees.

Dilution — Common law trademarks protect against the likelihood of confusion. So too does the Lanham Act. What is not protected is where a distinctive mark is used on unrelated products. For years state anti-dilution statues have provided causes of action to protect distinctive marks from encroachment, notwithstanding an absence of competition or the absence of confusion as to the source of goods or service. Now there is a federal dilution stature as well. Dilution is limited to famous marks and provides a basis for obtaining injunctive relief. Dilution protects against a proliferation of similar marks on unrelated goods or services. You can bring a dilution action regardless of lack of competition or likelihood of confusion.

Drawings — A drawing is the representation of a trademark as used on or in connection with the goods and comprises part of the trademark application. Drawings must be made with pen and ink or by a process that will produce high definition on reproduction. There are two types of drawings commonly used in trademark applications: typed drawings and computer-generated drawings. Typed drawings are always in all capital letters. Computer drawings show the mark how it appears on a specimen, or show the mark in some stylized form or design. Typed drawings are generally preferable since they are easier to prepare and cover all forms of the mark.

Generic names or descriptive term are usually deleted. Color is optional and is shown by the use of coded line drawings.

Federal Trademarks — Federal trademarks result from filing trademark applications under the Lanham Act. There are two registers — the Principal Register and the Supplemental Register. Types of marks available include trademarks, service marks, certification marks and collective marks. Filing is constructive use and notice of the applicant's claim to the mark. Before a trademark can be obtained, the applicant must provide proof of use in interstate or foreign commerce. However, by filing on an intent to use basis, proof of use can be delayed until after examination and publication. This allows the applicant to see what rights he or she will be granted and to find out whether any third parties will oppose before bringing out the trademarked product or service. A registration preempts the entire U.S. and is retroactive to the filing date for priority purposes. Registrations have ten year terms and are renewable.

Genericness — A trademark can become generic when it loses its ability to indicate a source of origin. When a substantial segment of the public thinks of a term as representing the object instead of being a trademark, it is generic and anyone can use it. To prevent trademarks from becoming generic, they should always be used as adjectives instead of nouns, and written or typed in a special form, e.g., with an initial or all-capital letters helps, and with a trademark indicator, e.g. the "Circle R " symbol.

Goodwill — By marketing goods, or providing services under a trademark, the trademark owner acquires certain protectable intangible property rights, referred to as "goodwill." It takes time and effort to build goodwill, and it can sometimes be destroyed overnight. Goodwill becomes associated with the trademark and must be included when the trademark is sold or the transfer is void. However, there is more to transferring goodwill than making a recital, and the business or tangible assets associated with the trademark should be transferred as well. If the purchaser is already in business, then less is required from the assignor. The key is for the public to receive the same quality goods before and after the sale. The responsibility is the buyer's to get whatever assets are required to achieve this goal.

Intent to Use — Prior to November 16, 1989, trademark applications which were filed with the U.S. Patent and Trademark Office had to be based on actual use in commerce. This meant that proof of use had to be submitted when the application was filed. With the passage of the Trademark Act of 1988, filings can now be made by stating an intention to use the mark and filing on the Principal Register. This allows a party to establish a priority date and have the mark examined and published for opposition before providing proof of use. (See Chapter Five.)

Mark — The term "mark" includes any trademark, service mark, collective mark or certification mark.

Notice of Registration — Federal registrations including both marks on the Principal and Supplemental Registers can be marked with statutory notations. Several versions are permitted. The most commonly used form is the ® or "Circle R." This should never be used with an unregistered mark, since this would be construed as fraud on the Trademark Office. Also, the "Circle R" should only be used in connection with the goods or services for which the mark is registered. If a notice of registration is used with the mark, the registrant is not precluded from recovering profits and damages in an infringement suit. Sometimes a TM or SM symbol, to mean trademark or service mark, are seen. These are non-statutory. The only purpose they serve is to make the mark distinctive.

Oppositions — Oppositions allow members of the public who can show special harm to second guess the examiner and object to the issuance of registrations which they do not think should have been allowed. When a trademark is published in the *Official Gazette*, parties having standing (who would suffer some direct harm) are able to file notice of opposition upon payment of a fee. Notice of opposition must be filed within 30 days. However, extensions up to 120 days from the date of publication may be taken. Usually, the grounds of opposition are because of alleged confusing similarity with a mark or name used by the opposer. Another common ground for opposition is descriptiveness. Marks on the Supplemental Register cannot be opposed. An inter partes action determines the registrability of the mark. (See Chapter Ten.)

Proof of Use — "Proof of use" means providing evidence of use of a trademark in connection with the claimed goods or services in a form acceptable to the U.S. Patent and Trademark Office. Proof of use is provided as part of the application if a use-based application is filed. Proof of use is required in connection with the Affidavit of Use or Amendment to Allege Use required for intent to use applications. Proof of use is also required in connection with Section 8 Declarations and for trademark renewals. For new applications, three proofs are required per class, which can be the same or different. For Section 8 Declarations and renewals, only a single proof of use per class is required. The proof should show the mark on the goods or packaging. For service marks, proofs can be photographs of signage, newspaper adds, billboard signs, radio and television adds, etc.

Publication — Once an application filed on the Principal Register has been found to be allowable by the Examiner, it goes to publication. Each week an *Official Gazette* is published which contains drawings of trademarks approved for publication. If someone wants to oppose issuance of a mark, there is a thirty-day time window. Upon motion, this can be increased in increments of thirty days for 120 days from publication.

Principal Register — When applications are filed on the Principal Register, there is automatic statutory notice. This precludes anyone from adopting and using the mark in good faith. Also, marks on the Principal Register can become incontestable after five years of continuous use. When a registration becomes incontestable, it cannot be attacked based on prior use or descriptiveness. Finally, marks on the Principal Register are presumed to be valid.

Quality Control — If the goods or services are provided directly by the trademark owner, quality control is inherent, because the owner purchases the raw materials, manufactures the products and does the design work, advertising and marketing. If a wholly-owned subsidiary is involved, control by the parent is assumed. If a trademark is used by an affiliate or licensed, there should be a formal license agreement. It is the affiliate or licensee which produces and markets the goods, and the owner exercises quality control by setting standards and performing inspections. The owner should have control over the mark on paper and also exercise actual on-site control.

Registered Mark — A mark registered in the U.S. Patent and Trademark Office.

Related Company — The term "related company" means any person whose use of a mark is controlled by the owner of the mark with respect to the nature and quality of the goods or services on or in connection with which the mark is used. If a trademark is used by a related company, rights inure to the benefit of the owner of the mark. The key word here is "controlled." If a company is 100 percent owned, it is controlled. Otherwise, a license agreement with quality control provisions is required to show the right of control.

Renewals — Trademark registrations last so long as they are maintained. Renewal is required every ten years. The owner pays a fee and provides proof of use during the six month period before the expiration of the term, or by paying an additional fee, within three months after the expiration date. If the renewal is not made, the registration will lapse. However, this doesn't mean the trademark is abandoned. If the mark is still in use, the party will still have common law usage rights. If desired, the same or another party can register, since trademarks, unlike patents, are recyclable, and rights can be created anew.

Registrant — A person owning a federal trademark registration, including legal representatives, predecessors, successors and assigns of such registrant.

Section 8 Declarations — Section 8 Declarations are necessary to maintain a registration. A Section 8 Declaration confirms that the registrant is still using the mark for the designated goods and services and proof of use of the mark in commerce is provided. Section 8 Declarations must be filed during the sixth year of the registration. Normally, they are combined with a Section 15 Declaration. If the Section 8 Declaration is filed and accepted, the registration will continue for its full term of ten years.

Section 15 Declarations — A Section 15 Declaration makes a registration on the Principal Register incontestable. While a Section 15 Declaration can be filed anytime when there has been five years of continuous use, conventional practice is to file it with the Section 8 Declaration early during the sixth year of the Declaration. The strategy is to file when first permitted so that the registration becomes more defensible. This has no application to marks on the Supplemental Register, since they cannot become incontestable.

Service Mark — The term service mark means any word, name, symbol, or device, or any combination thereof, used by a person or which a person has a bona fide intent to use in commerce and applies to register on the Principal Register, which identifies and distinguishes the services of one person, including a unique service, from the services of others and to indicate the source of the services, even if that source is unknown.

Source of Origin — Trademarks indicate source of origin. Consumers buy goods or obtain services under a trademark or brand name because they expect to receive a certain quality of goods or performance. It is this assurance or expectation of repeatability of quality that causes customers to return. Consumers feel at ease buying a nationally-known trademarked product from the dealer which offers the lowest price because they expect consistent quality.

State Trademarks — All of the states have trademark laws. There is a uniform state law that many states have adopted. Other states have trademark laws with their own spin. The state registration process is not very substantive and the rights generally granted aren't any more significant than what the party possessed at common law. Also, since there is no examination except for form, validity is left for the courts.

Supplemental Register — The Supplemental Register allows registrations for descriptive marks that wouldn't be registrable on the Principal Register. However, since the Supplemental registrations cannot be opposed, they do not give statutory notice to third parties, and the registrant cannot make them incontestable. However, the registrant can use the "Circle R" symbol with the mark and can sue in federal court.

Trademark — The term "trademark" shall mean any word, name, symbol or device, or any combination thereof, used by a person, or which a person has a bona fide intent to use in commerce and applies to register on the Principal Register, which indemnifies and distinguishes his or her goods, including a unique product, from those manufactured and sold by others and to indicate source of origin of goods, even if that source is unknown.

Trade Name — The term "trade name" or "commercial name" means any name used by a person to identify his or her business or vocation. Trade names are not registrable under the Lanham Act.

Uncontrolled Licensing — A trademark owner has the duty to control the nature and quality of goods sold under his mark. When a trademark is licensed to another party, the licensor must exercise quality control of the goods produced. If the licensor fails to control quality, the mark may lose significance as an indication of origin and be found to have been abandoned.

United States — The United States includes all territory which is under its jurisdiction and control.

Use in Commerce — All federal law must be based on authority granted in the Constitution. Trademark law, like a number of other laws, is based on the Commerce Clause. A trademark can only be obtained if the mark has been used in foreign or interstate commerce. However, intent to use filings can be made, whereby proof of use is deferred until after notice of allowance. The law is very liberal in regard to what constitutes commerce. The term "use in commerce" means the bona fide use of a mark in ordinary course of trade and not made merely to reserve a right in the mark. A mark shall be deemed to be in use in commerce — (1) on goods, when (A) it is placed in any manner on the goods or their containers or the displays associated therewith or on the tags or labels affixed thereto, or if the nature of the goods makes such placement impractical, then on the documents associated with the goods or their sale, and (B) the goods are sold or transported in commerce, and (2) on services when it is used or displayed in the sale or advertising of services and the services are rendered in commerce, or the services are rendered more than one state, or in the United States and a foreign country, and the person rendering the services is engaged in commerce in connection with the services.

Index